Bloomin Gorgeous
patterns for living

Welcome to the fashion design sketchbook from Bloomin Gorgeous!

These amazing designs belong to

~~~~~~
~~~~~~

Contents of love!

<u>Everyone has a designer's touch</u>

Now and again, I find something in the high street stores that I really love. Most of the time I buy wardrobe staples like t-shirts and vest tops but don't really feel enthused about the statement items. This has been the same since my youth.

Now I can design and make my own clothes, I feel much freer to wear what I want and feel comfortable in what I wear. Having a few essential patterns helps when making clothes. It's always fun to create new and interesting pieces, inspired by, if not in loving adoration of, more runway worthy designer items.

You will see, in the short chapters at the beginning of this sketchbook, just how you can piece together an outfit, design new shapes to suit your figure and even think about what patterns may help you complete your design aspirations.

First things first, how do you design clothing? Well a model helps immensely…

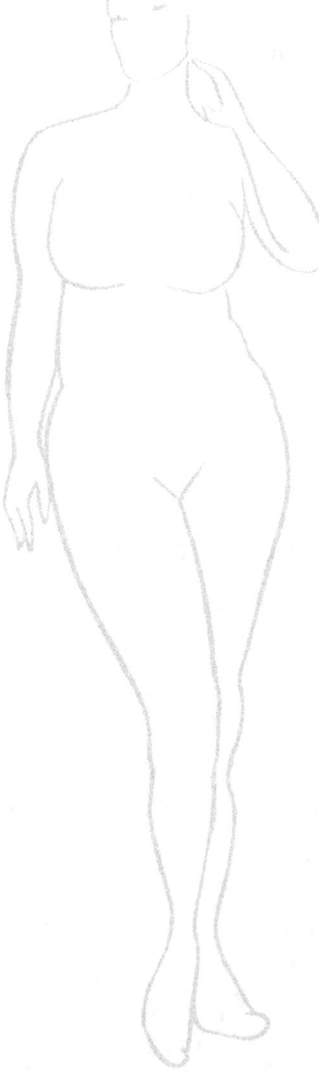

These two figures are called croquis. A croquis is a basic shape of a model that can be designed onto. This book contains croquis with guidelines and without; so if you need a little more help constructing your designs, the lines are there! When you get more confident, the croquis towards the back of the book no longer include guidelines.

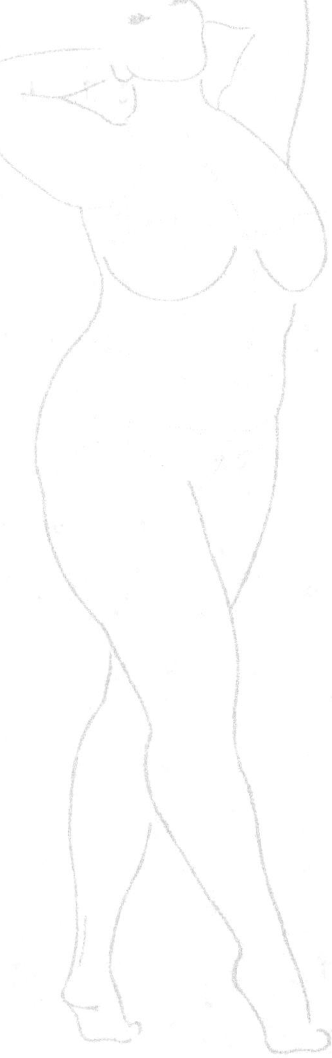

Fashion Fixtures

There are well known shapes and finishes that are used in design, many of them are reproduced endlessly in the recycling of fashion. We can use them in different combinations to help us come up with items that not only are individual but are more suited to our own individual body shapes. When you have something that works, wearing clothes becomes much more about confidence and not so much about just covering up.

Let's start at the top!

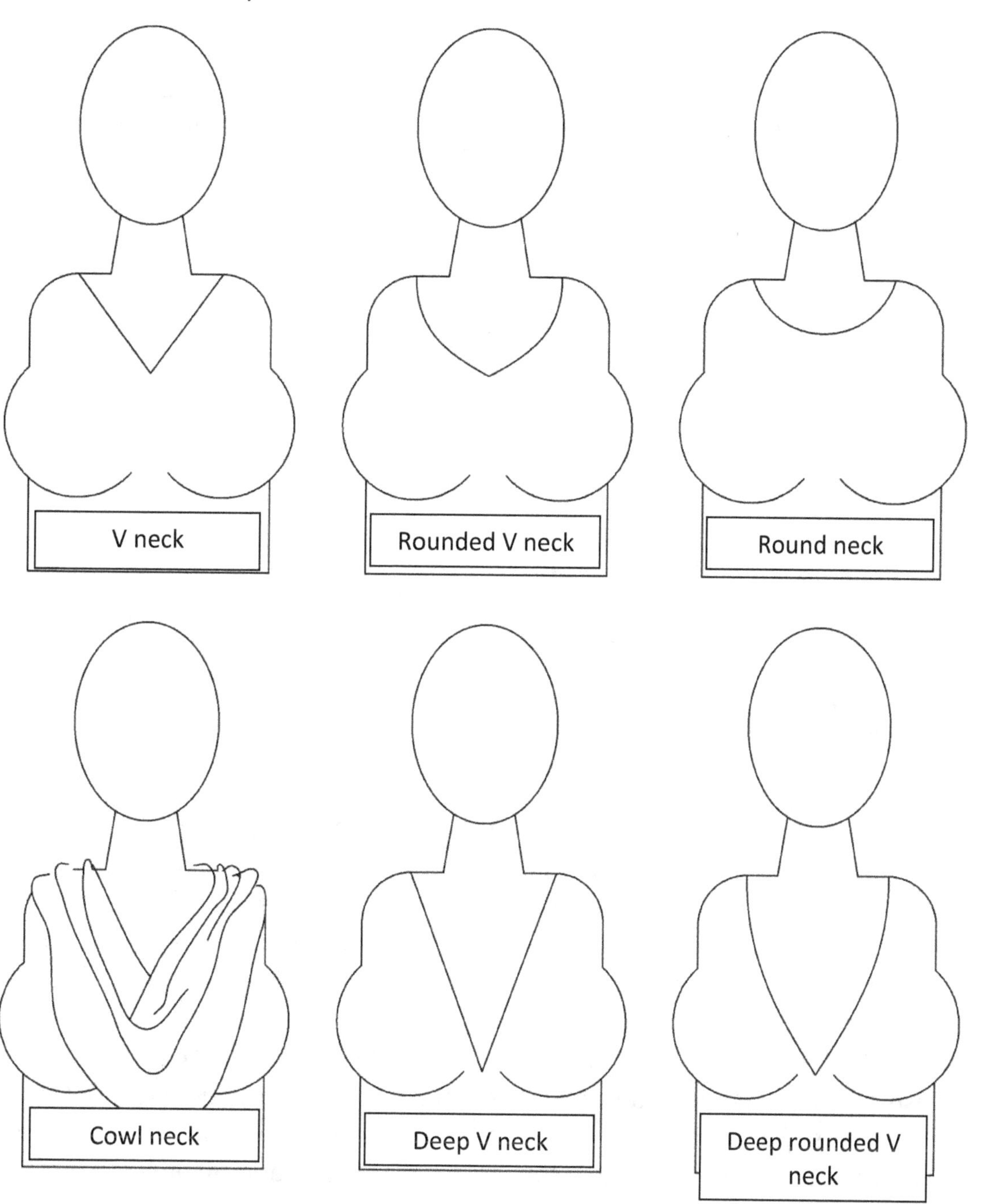

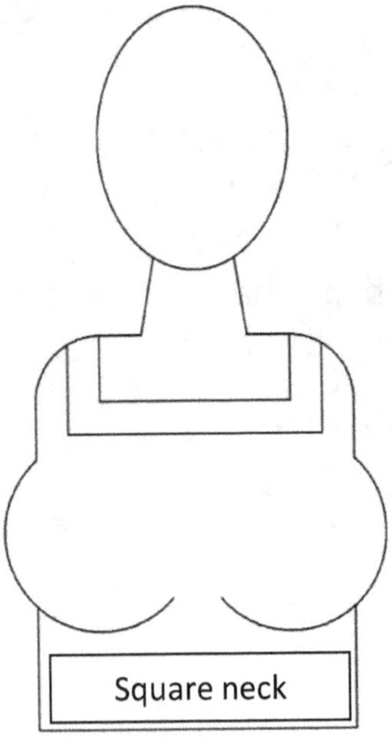

Square neck

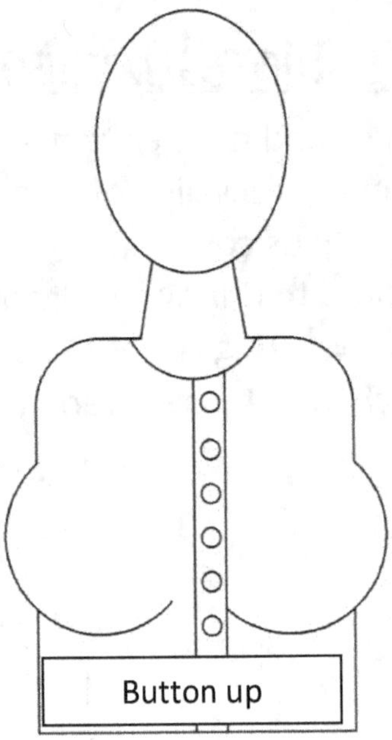

Button up

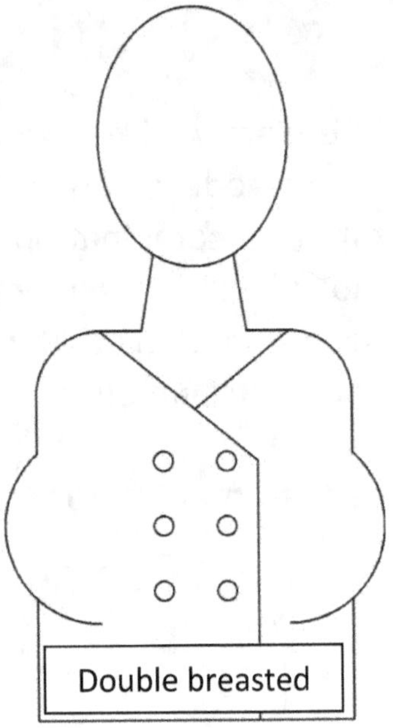

Double breasted

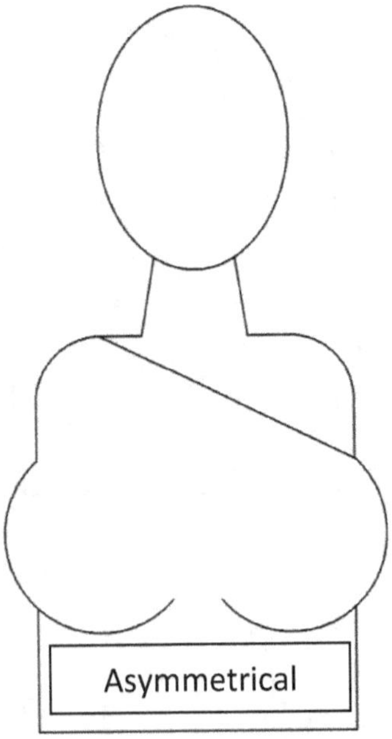

Asymmetrical

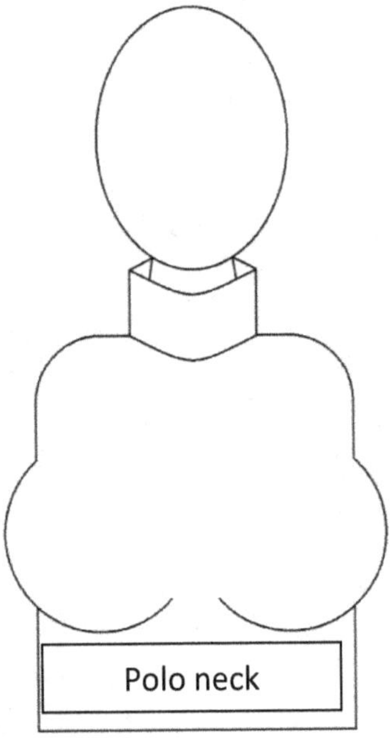

Polo neck

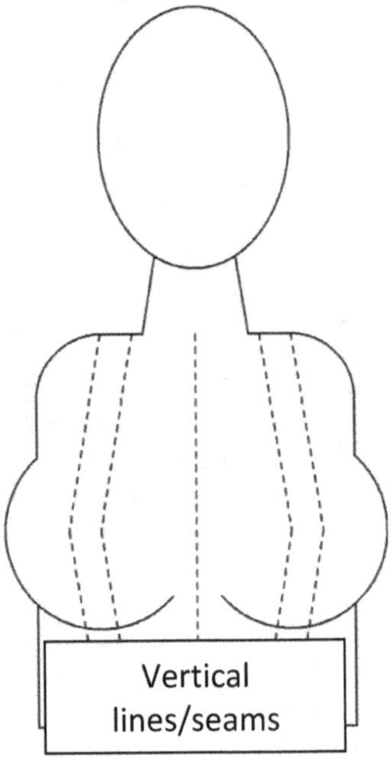

Vertical lines/seams

When it comes to shapes, if you like it use it! There shouldn't be any rules to design or fashion. You will however find lines and shapes that you feel most comfortable in. All body shapes are different, which is why I have included more than one shape in this sketchbook. It also pays to remember that a fuller bust will make straight lines more curved on the final figure, but this is no reason not to use them!

Fabric choice also plays a large part in what works well as a shape and what doesn't. Some patterned fabric is irresistible but may not drape well, some stretchy jersey or scuba fabric feels amazing to wear but would be no use when structure is required! Be sure to take this into consideration when you are thinking about making your designs a reality.

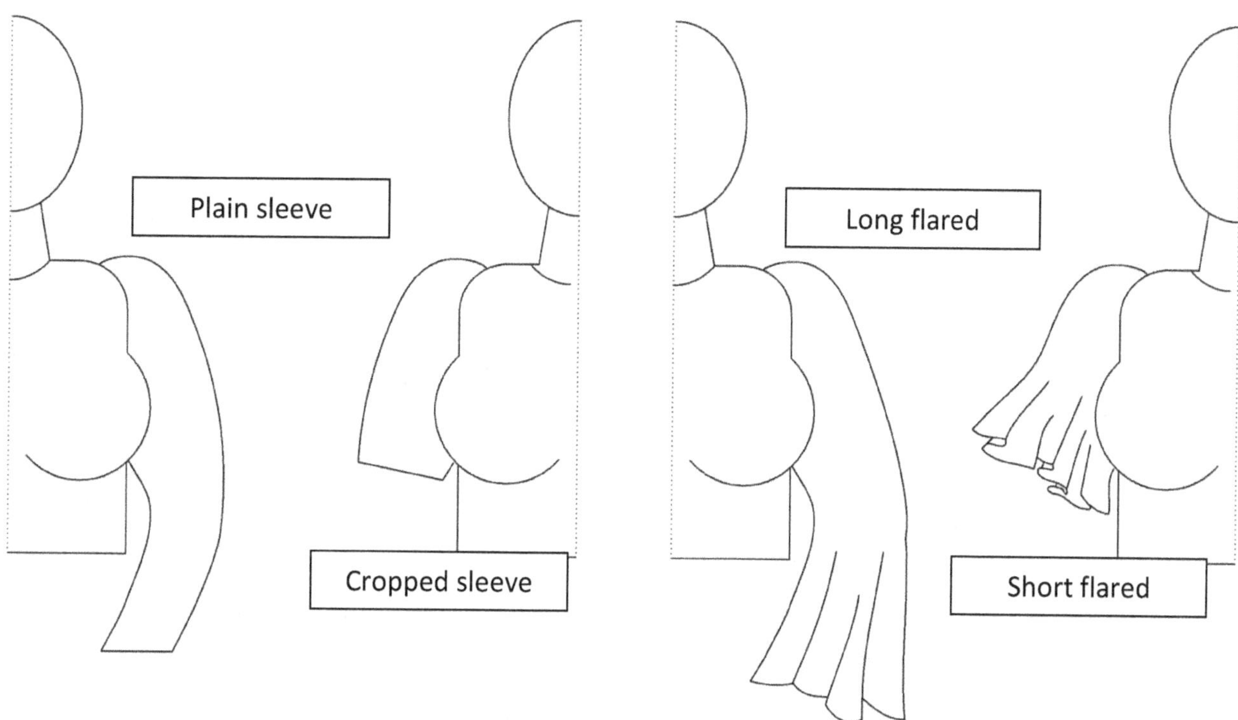

Sleeves can make a huge difference to a top. They can disguise large shoulders, or tighten an upper arm. They can balance out a shape and add interest in an instant. Sleeves, when paired with different neck and body lines and shapes, ensure an almost endless amount of combinations and designs.

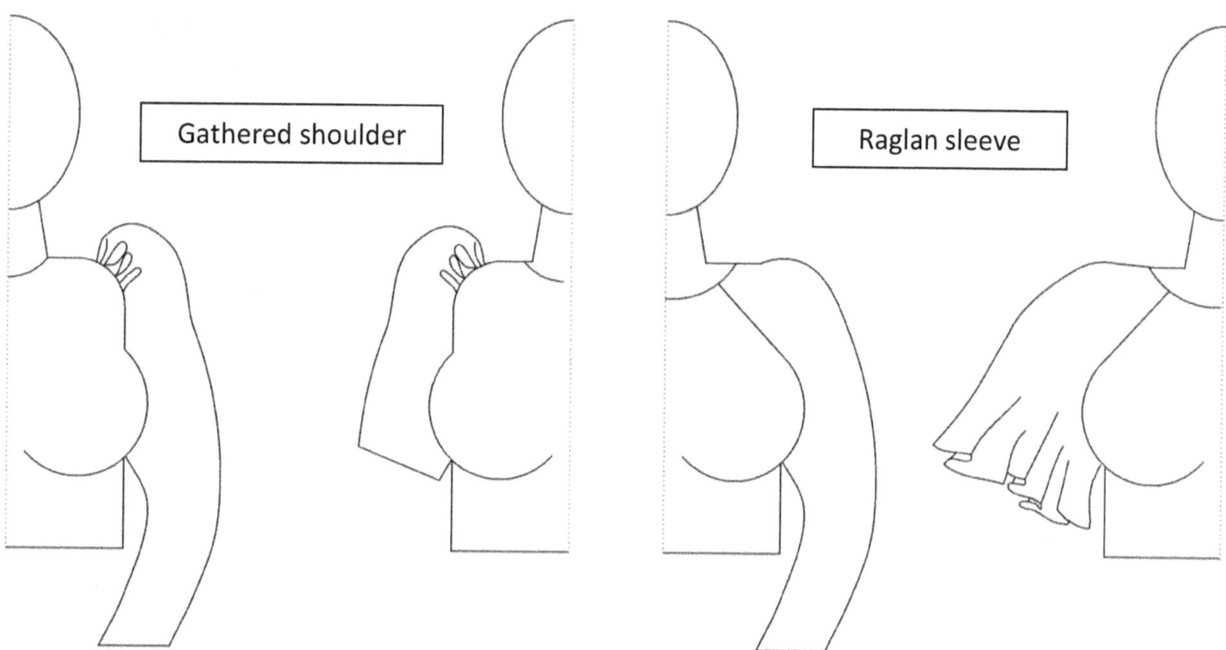

Fabric choice again plays a large part in how well a design works. Well draping fabric creates fabulous ruffles and flares. Stiffer fabric works well in gathered shoulders and sleeves with structural seams.

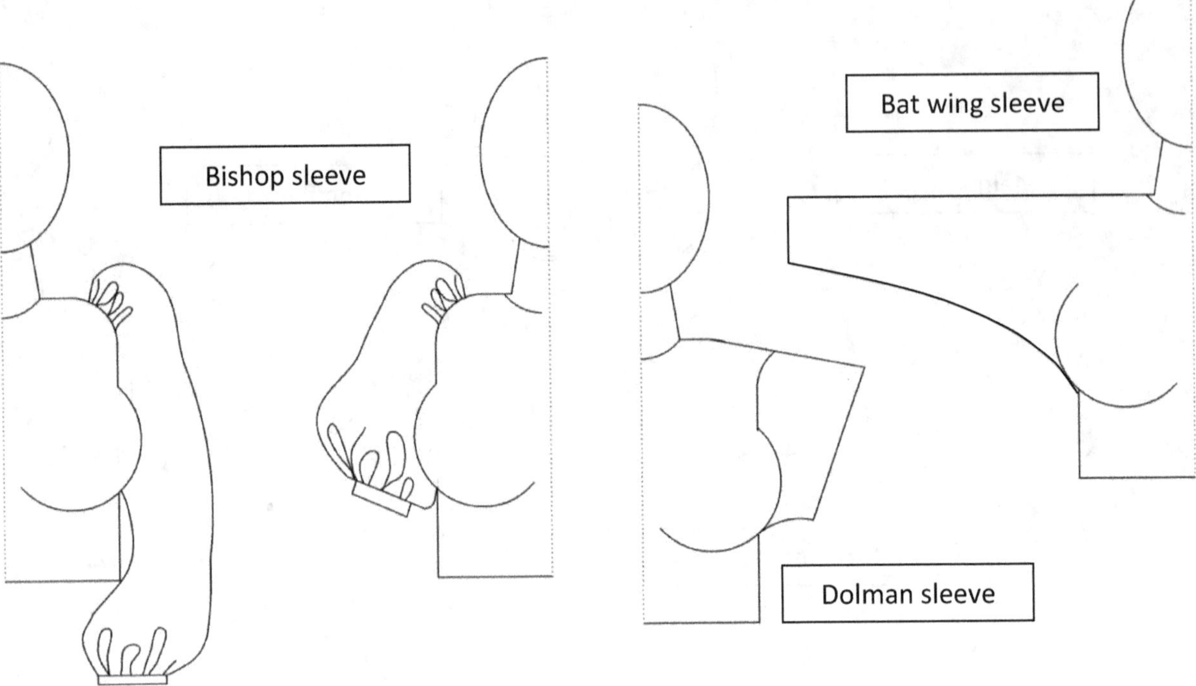

When it comes to sleeves there are many more varieties than I can show here but this is a good start and includes the most commonly used shapes and arm structures.

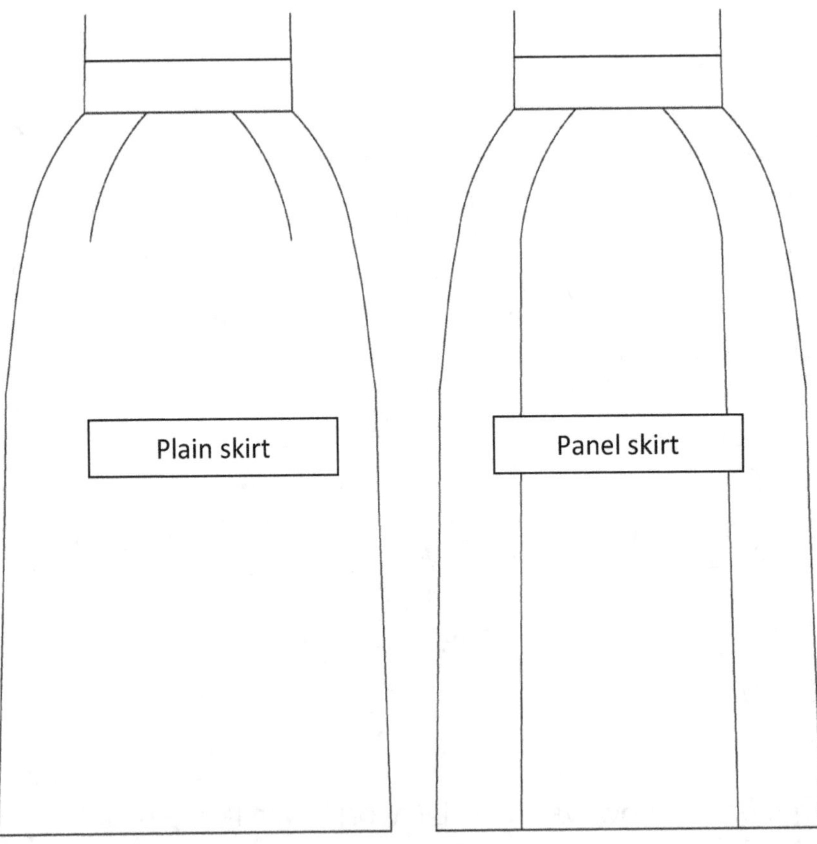

Next comes the bottom half. Again, there are endless variations to be made to the same themes and shapes. I have included just a few to help you make a start on your designing journey. In this image the same shape of skirt is accomplished in different ways. This can become much more than structural when colours and fabrics are taken into consideration.

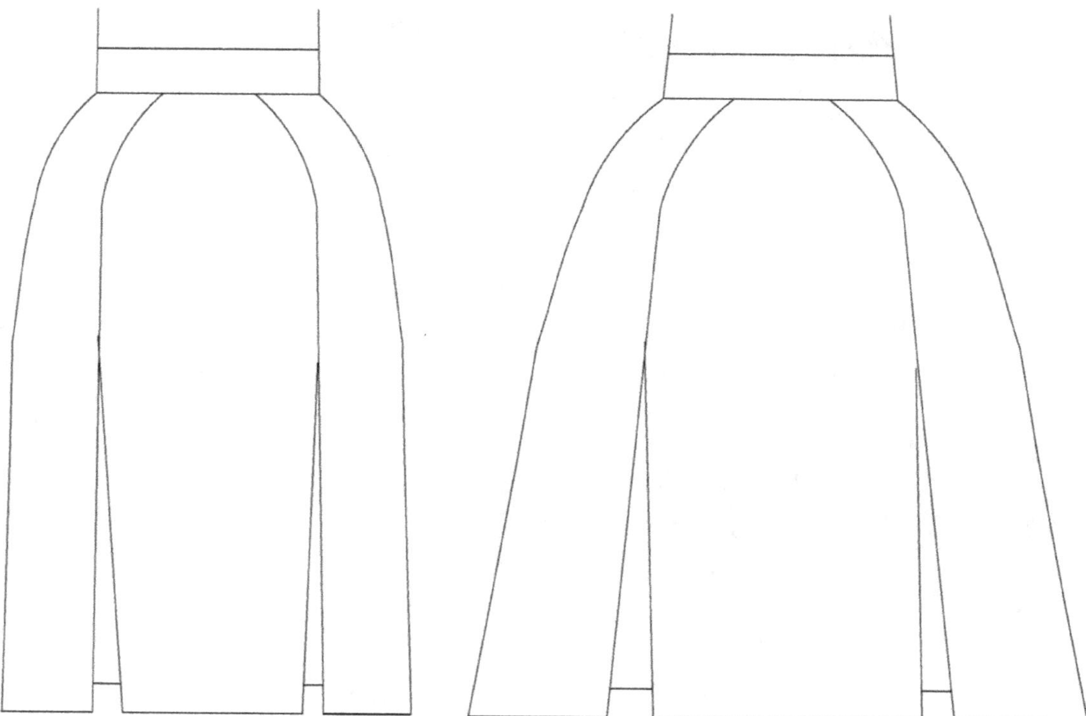

Adding in extra pleats of fabric can really create movement and space. It is also a really great way of adding a dash of colour to be revealed only when you are in motion. A godet can also be added, this is similar to a pleat, but is visible as part of the skirt all the time.

Gathers can add fullness to the waist and add character and shape. These can take the form of free gathers all around the skirt waist or can just be in certain areas. Once again, all of the structures and shapes can be affected by the fabric choice and will be less effective if the fabric is not suited to the need.

If an A line skirt was made of a thick canvas it would end up looking like this.

This skirt could be made with a circle, plain pieces or even panels.

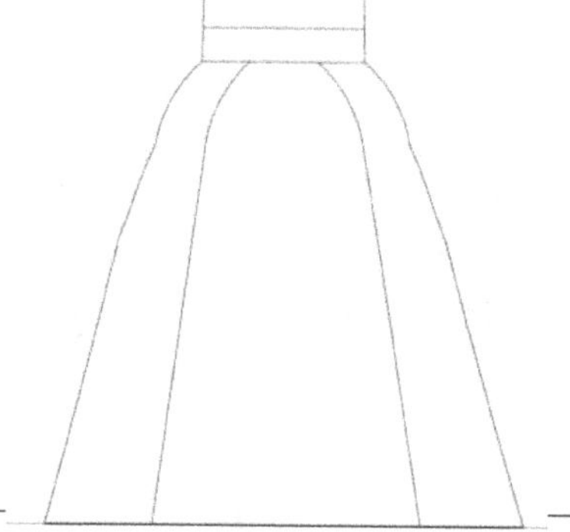

Where to get inspiration

Inspiration can come from absolutely anywhere. If you see a cloud formation you like, if you are interested in plants, even if you love stationary, you can be inspired to design. Let's take an extreme example, shall we?

Here is an image of some railings. I like the formal structure of the lines and repetitions with just a couple of the railings having the extra bulbus part in the center.

I like the way the light plays on the rounded surfaces and how that is juxtaposed with the straight lines and edges of the rails.

I can take inspiration from the straight lines and the curves.

I can think about how this might create structure in a design, or how it might influence a fabric choice.

I can trace from this very image and use the shapes directly on a design of my own.

I can even cut this image out, stick it, or parts of it, directly onto my croquis. I can then go in and add extra sketches if needed.

You can see the straight-line influence on this design in the straps holding a wide neckline in place.

The figure-hugging skirt helps create the rounded structure.

A high shine lurex fabric or even faux leather could work really well for the skirt.
A short pile velvet or plain good quality jersey for the top.

Measurements and where to take them

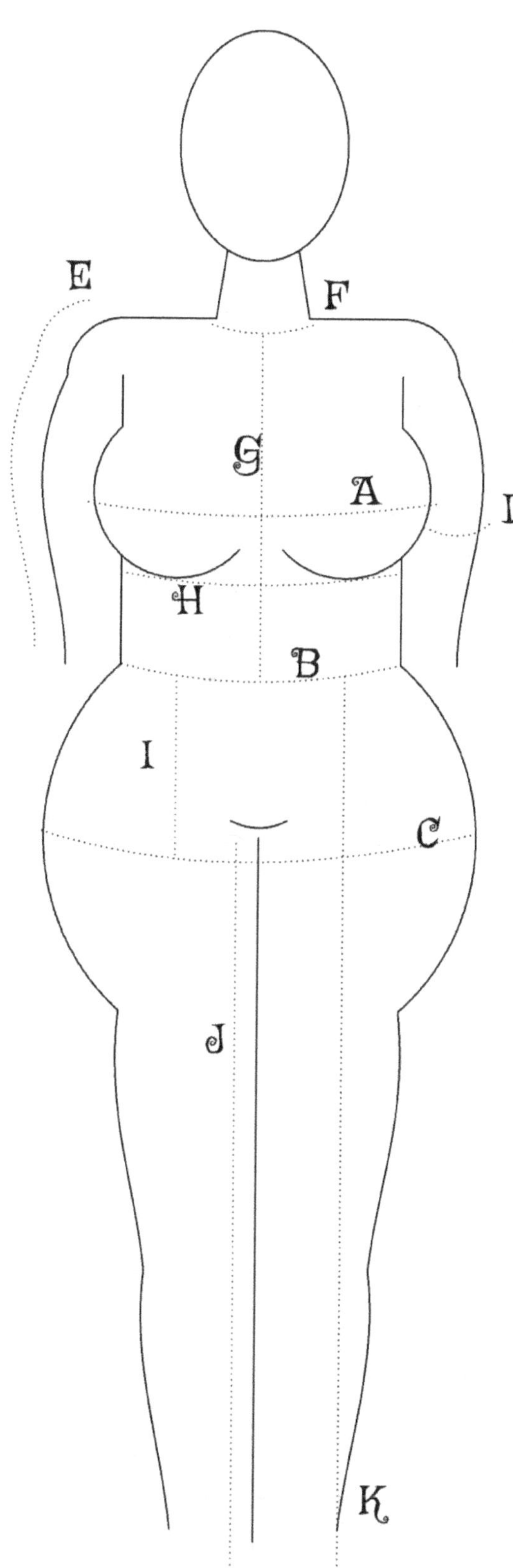

A= Bust circumference
B= Waist circumference
C= Hips circumference
D= Arm girth
E= Arm length
F= Neck circumference
G= Neck to waist (down your back)
H= Under bust circumference
I= Waist to hip
J= Inside leg length
K= Waist to ankle

Generally, the only measurements you need to know when shopping online are the 'Bust', the 'Waist' and the 'Hips measurements. When choosing patterns, this remains generally the same. However, it can be really useful to know more measurements when using patterns so that you can adjust them to fit you better. You might even 'hack' a pattern to change it. At 'Bloomin Gorgeous Patterns' we like to think about size slightly differently so you won't find any numbers in our size names!

Measurements tables for your reference

Measurements for (name)	
Bust	
Waist	
Hips	
Arm girth	
Arm length	
Neck circumference	
Neck to waist	
Under bust	
Waist to hip	
Inside leg	
Waist to ankle	

Measurements for (name)	
Bust	
Waist	
Hips	
Arm girth	
Arm length	
Neck circumference	
Neck to waist	
Under bust	
Waist to hip	
Inside leg	
Waist to ankle	

Measurements for (name)	
Bust	
Waist	
Hips	
Arm girth	
Arm length	
Neck circumference	
Neck to waist	
Under bust	
Waist to hip	
Inside leg	
Waist to ankle	

Measurements for (name)	
Bust	
Waist	
Hips	
Arm girth	
Arm length	
Neck circumference	
Neck to waist	
Under bust	
Waist to hip	
Inside leg	
Waist to ankle	

Measurements for (name)	
Bust	
Waist	
Hips	
Arm girth	
Arm length	
Neck circumference	
Neck to waist	
Under bust	
Waist to hip	
Inside leg	
Waist to ankle	

Measurements for (name)	
Bust	
Waist	
Hips	
Arm girth	
Arm length	
Neck circumference	
Neck to waist	
Under bust	
Waist to hip	
Inside leg	
Waist to ankle	

The Bloomin Gorgeous approach to dress size

Your size	Bust cm	Waist cm	Hips cm	Arm Girth cm
Glorious	80	64	88	26
Awesome	84	68	92	27.2
Magnificent	88	72	96	28.4
Superb	92	76	100	29.6
Fabulous	96	80	104	30.8
Sensational	100	84	108	32
Fantastic	104	88	112	33.2
Delightful	110	94	117	35.2
Lovely	116	100	122	37.2
Stunning	122	106	127	39.2
Captivating	128	112	132	41.2
Enchanting	134	118	137	43.2
Spectacular	140	124	142	45.2
Gorgeous	146	130	147	47.2
Sensuous	152	136	152	49.2
Luscious	158	142	157	51.2
Voluptuous	164	148	162	53.2
Terrific	170	154	167	55.2
Wonderful	176	160	172	57.2

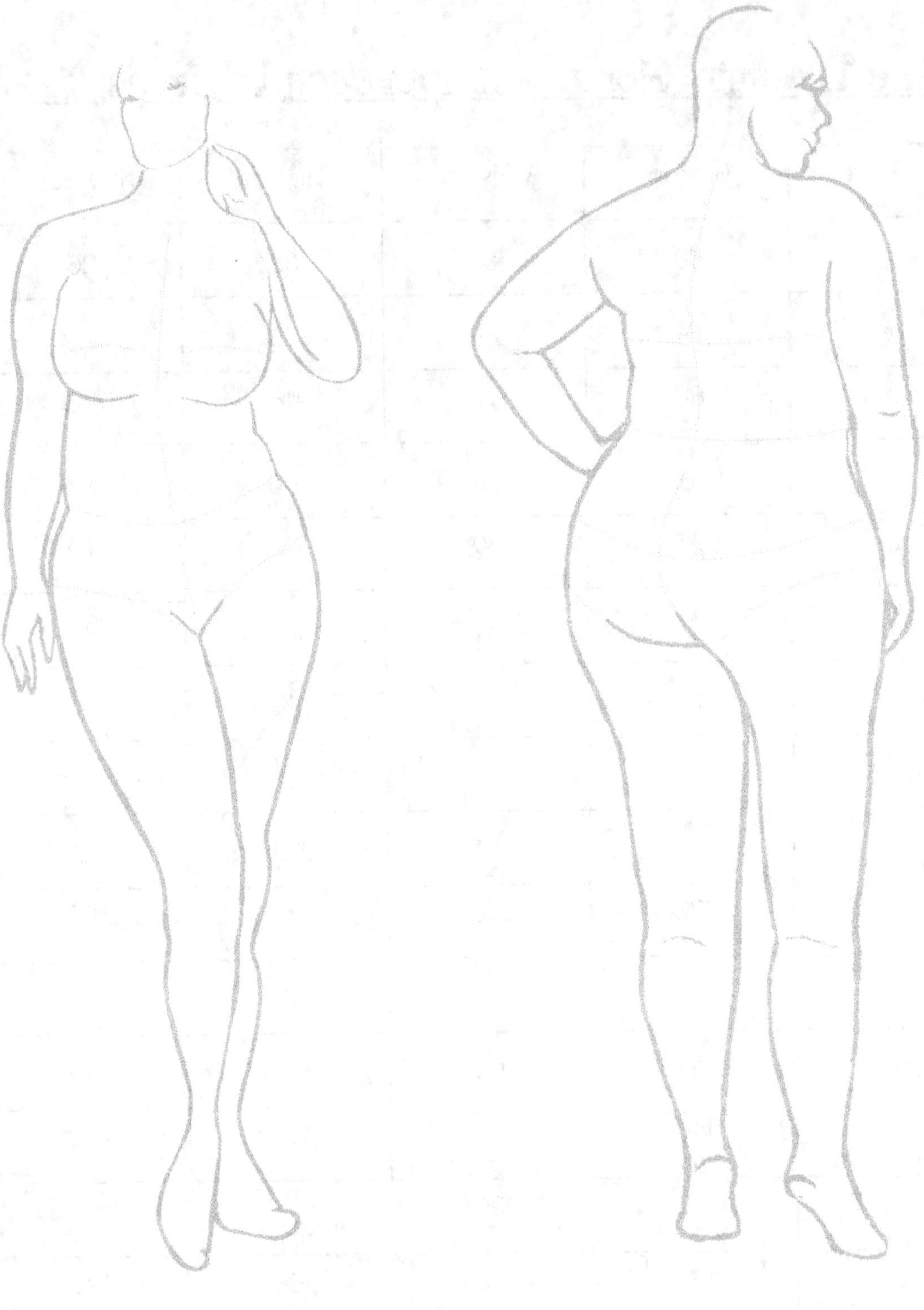

NOTES

NOTES

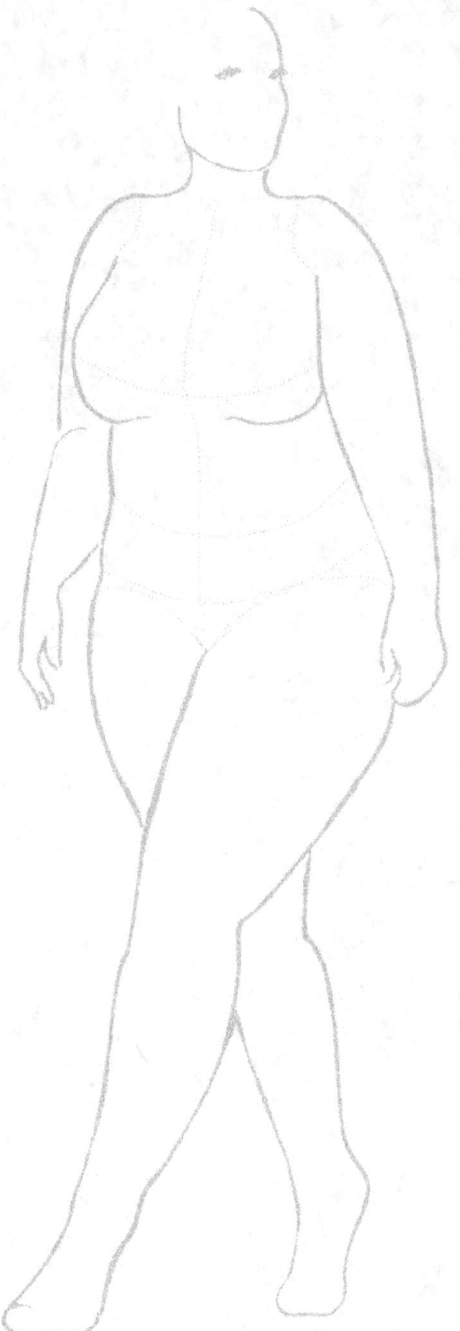

NOTES____

____

____

____

____

____

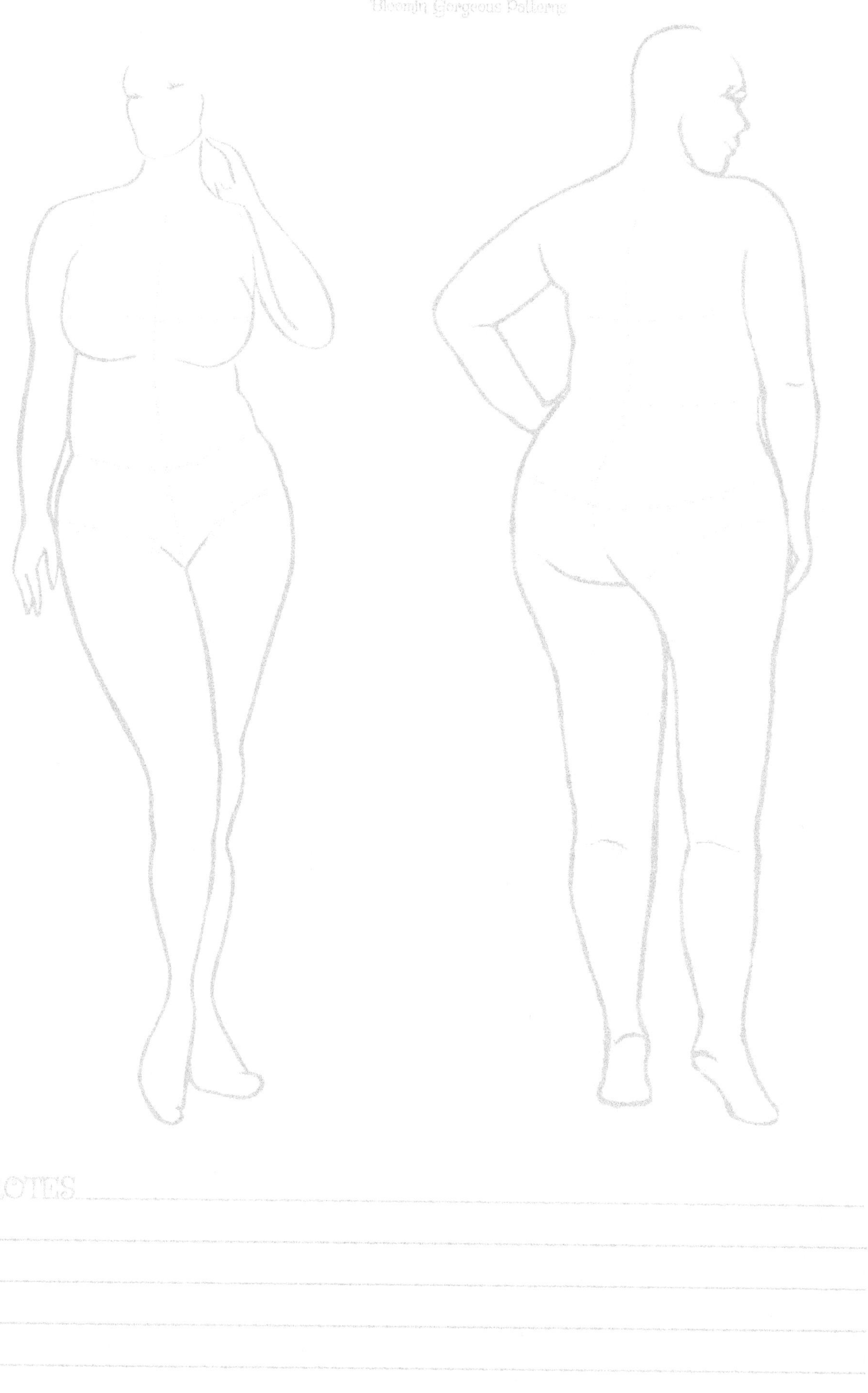

NOTES
____
____
____
____
____
____

NOTES____

____

____

____

____

____

NOTES

NOTES ____
____
____
____
____
____

NOTES

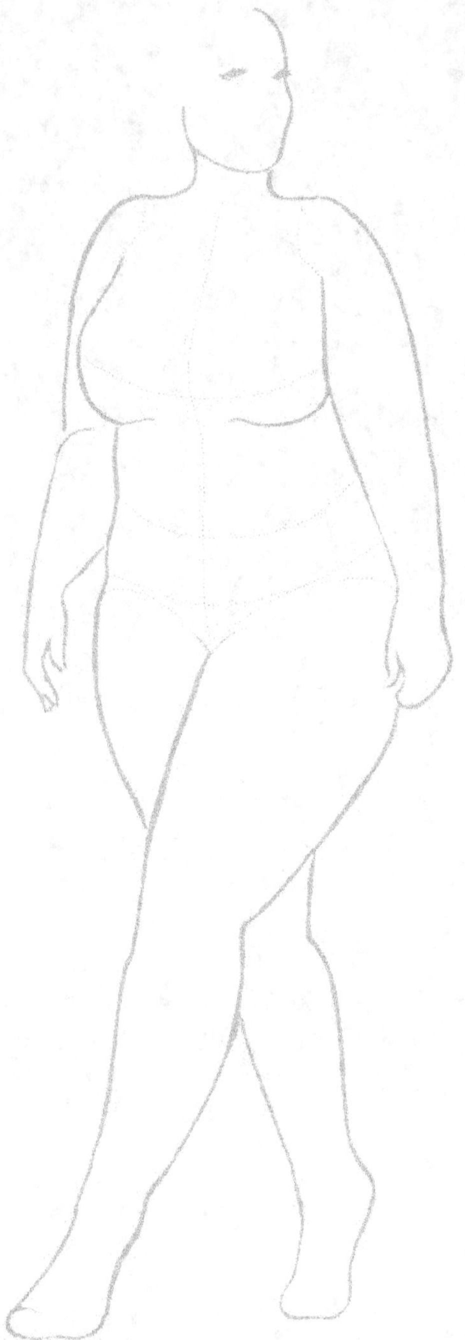

NOTES

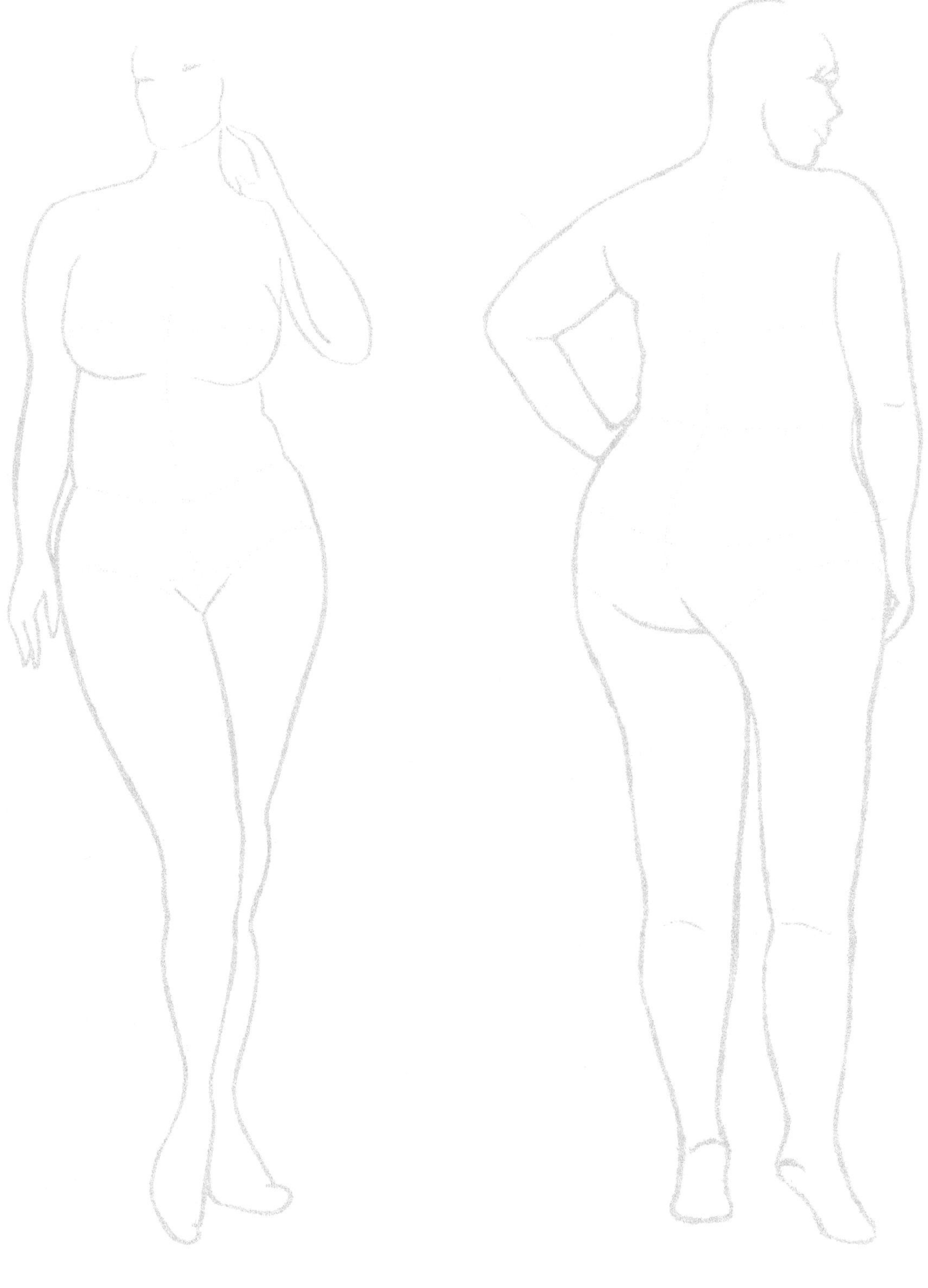

NOTES

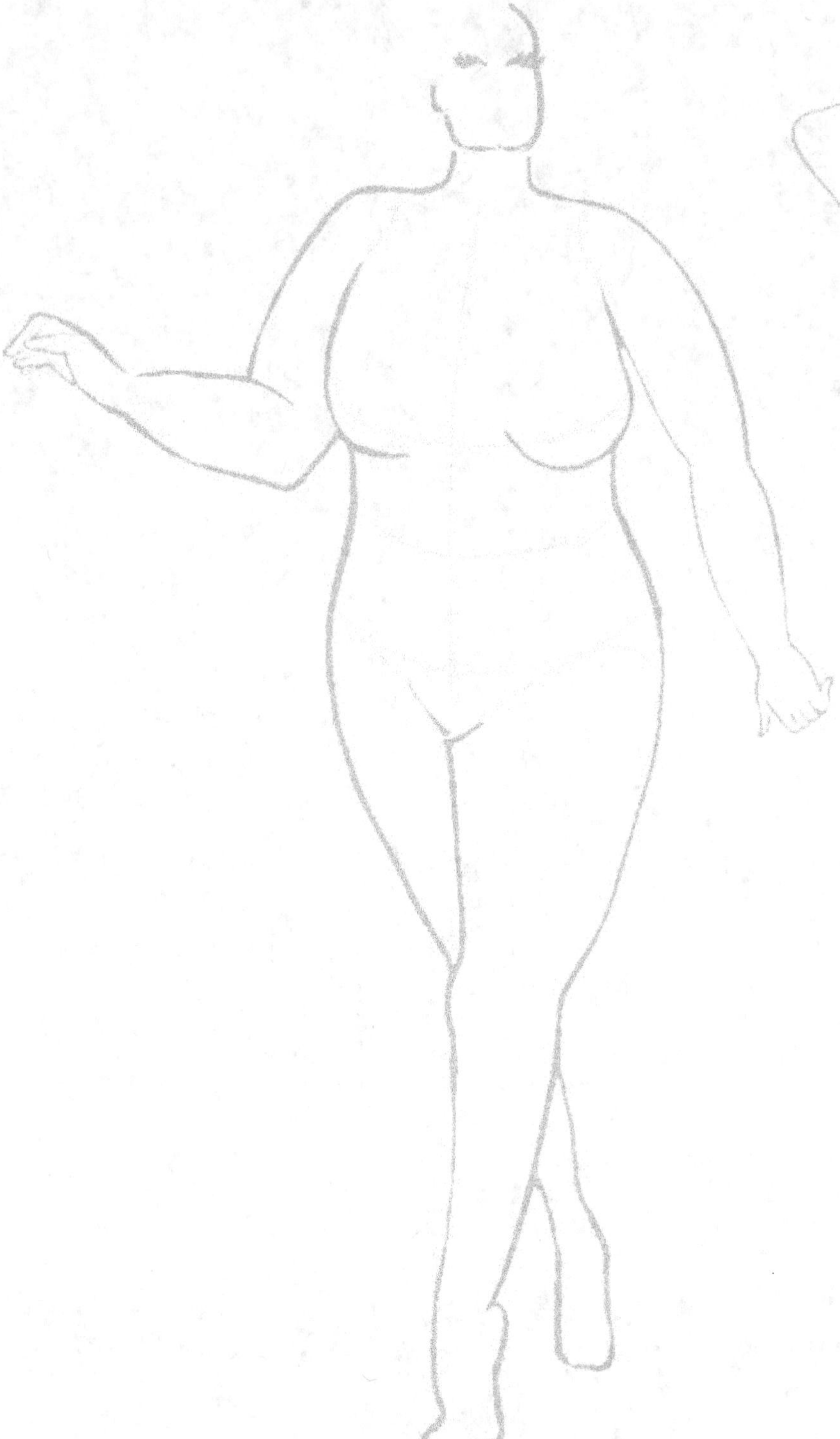

NOTES____

____

____

____

____

____

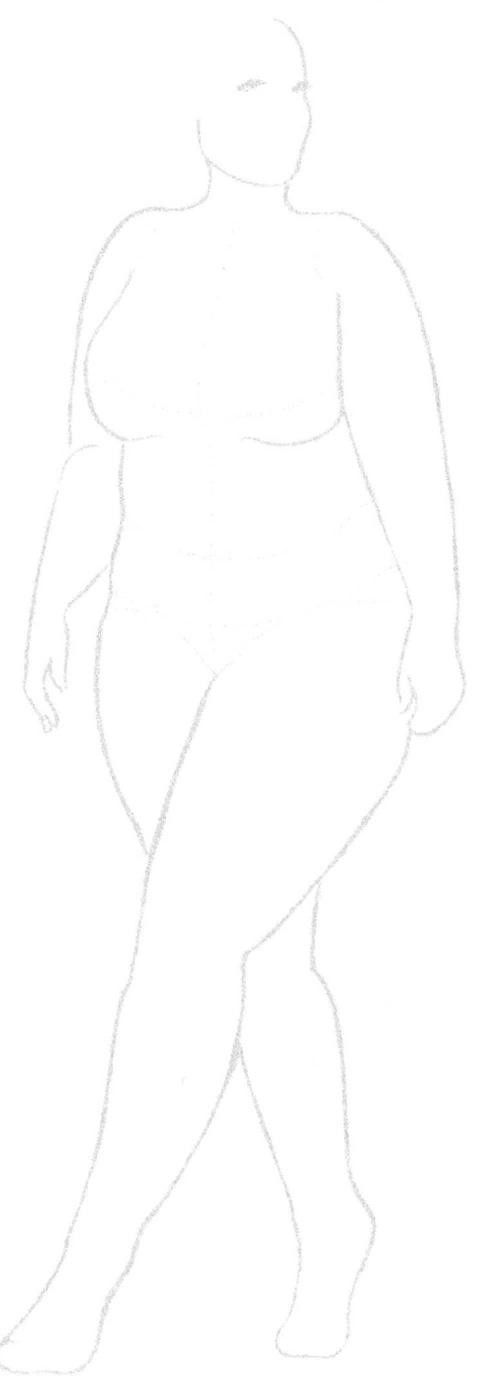

NOTES

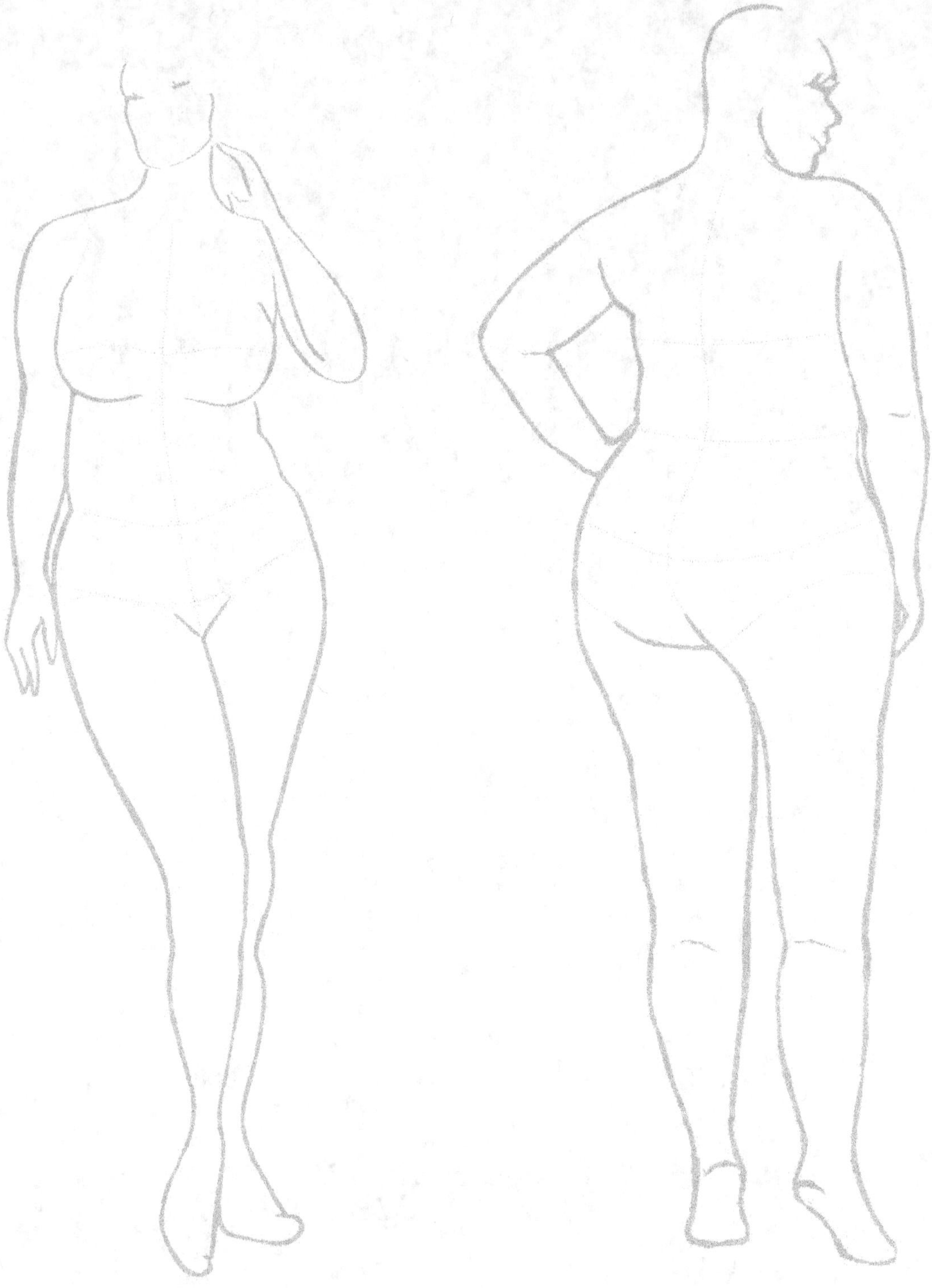

NOTES____

____

____

____

____

____

NOTES

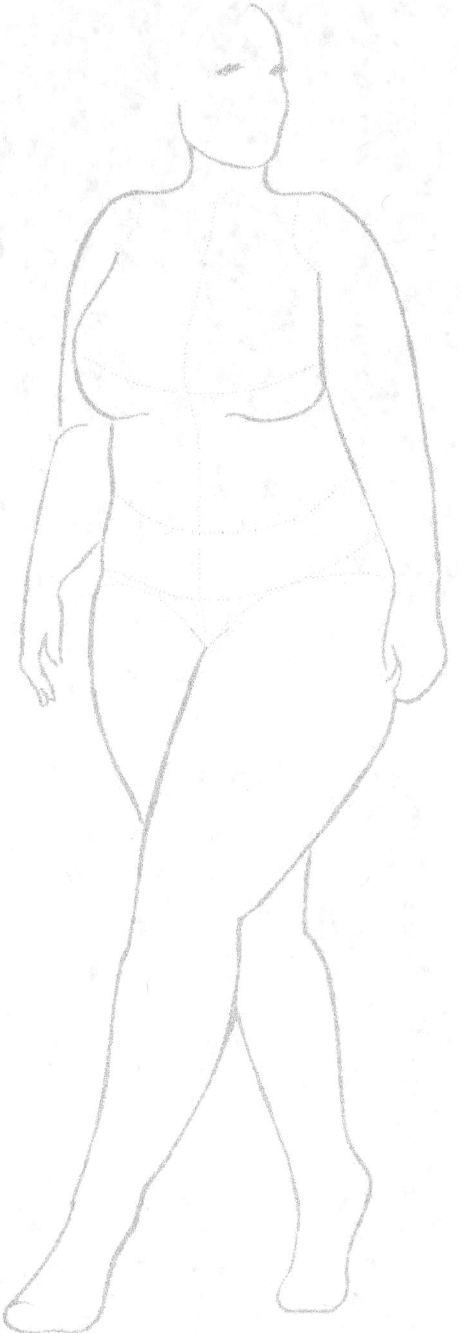

NOTES

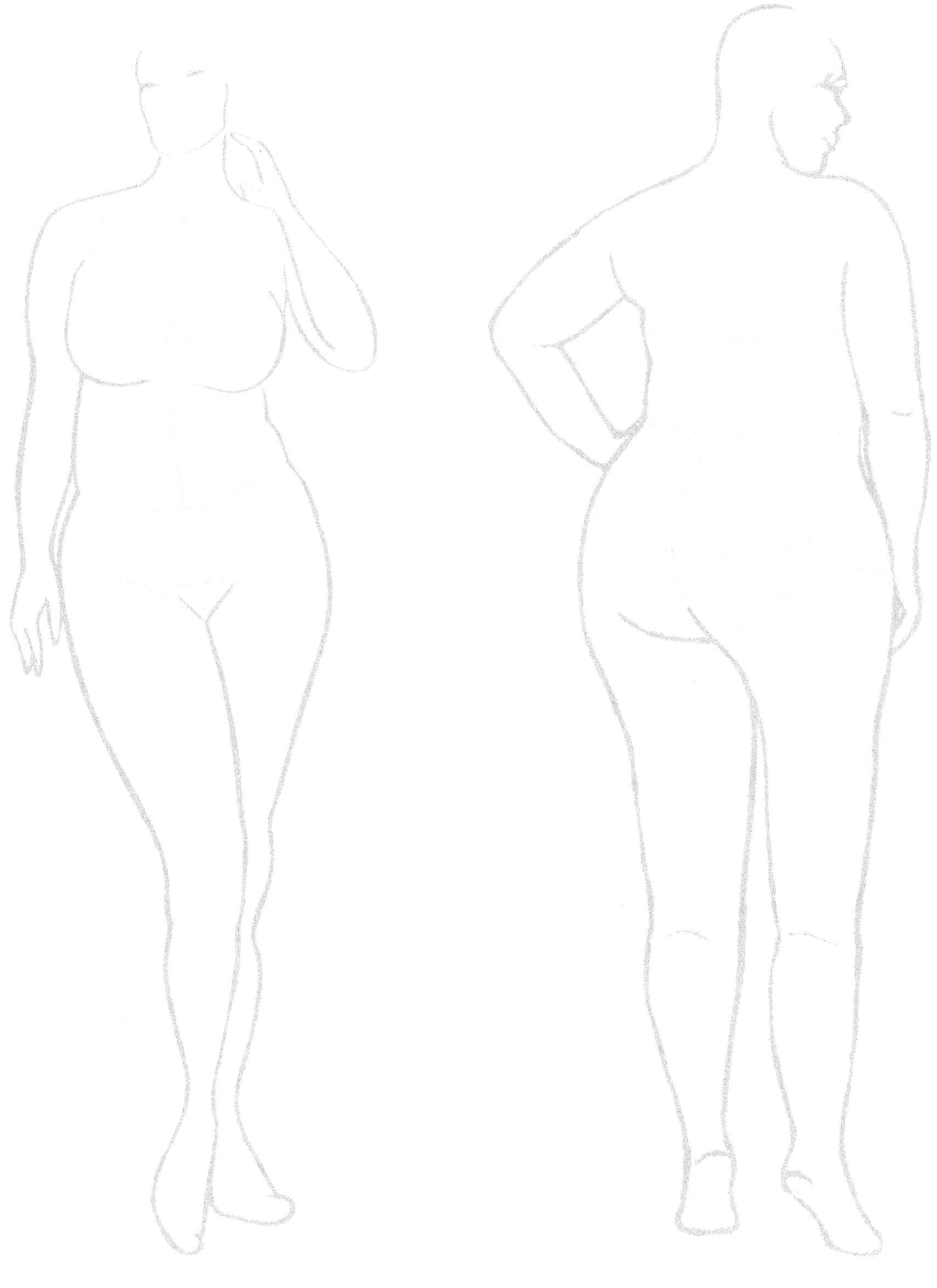

NOTES

NOTES____

____

____

____

____

____

NOTES

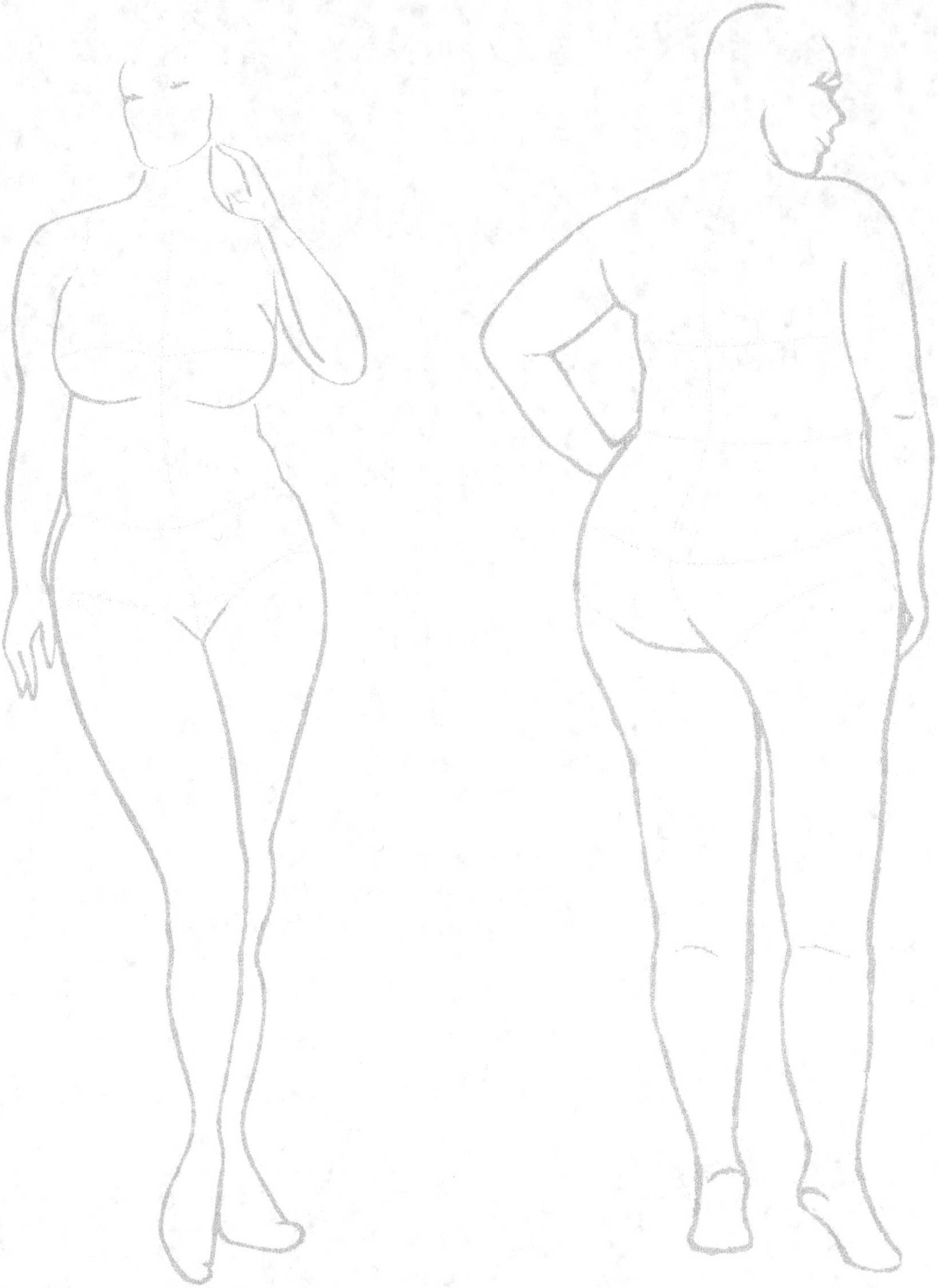

NOTES

NOTES

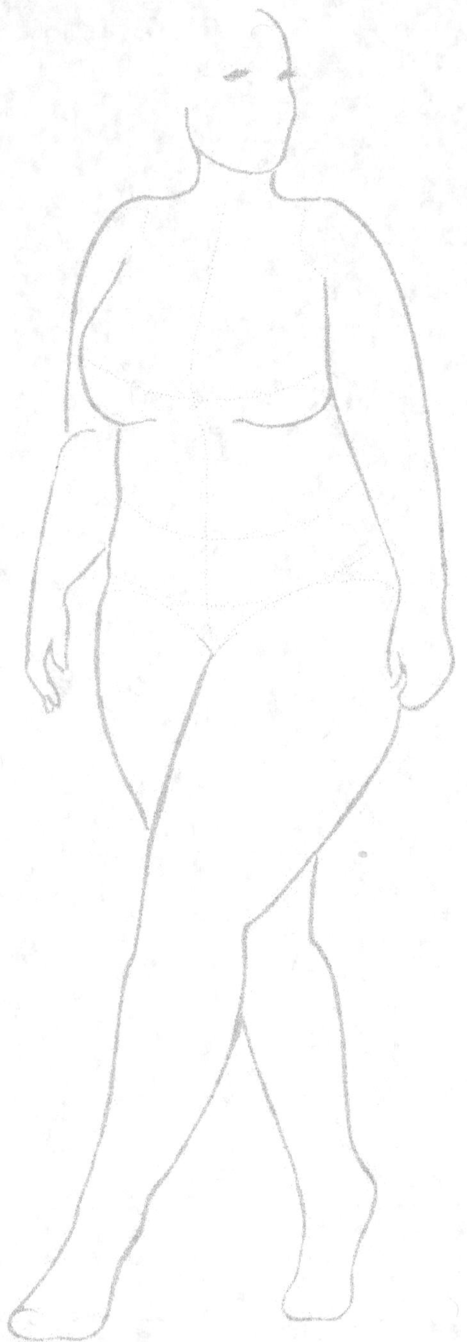

NOTES

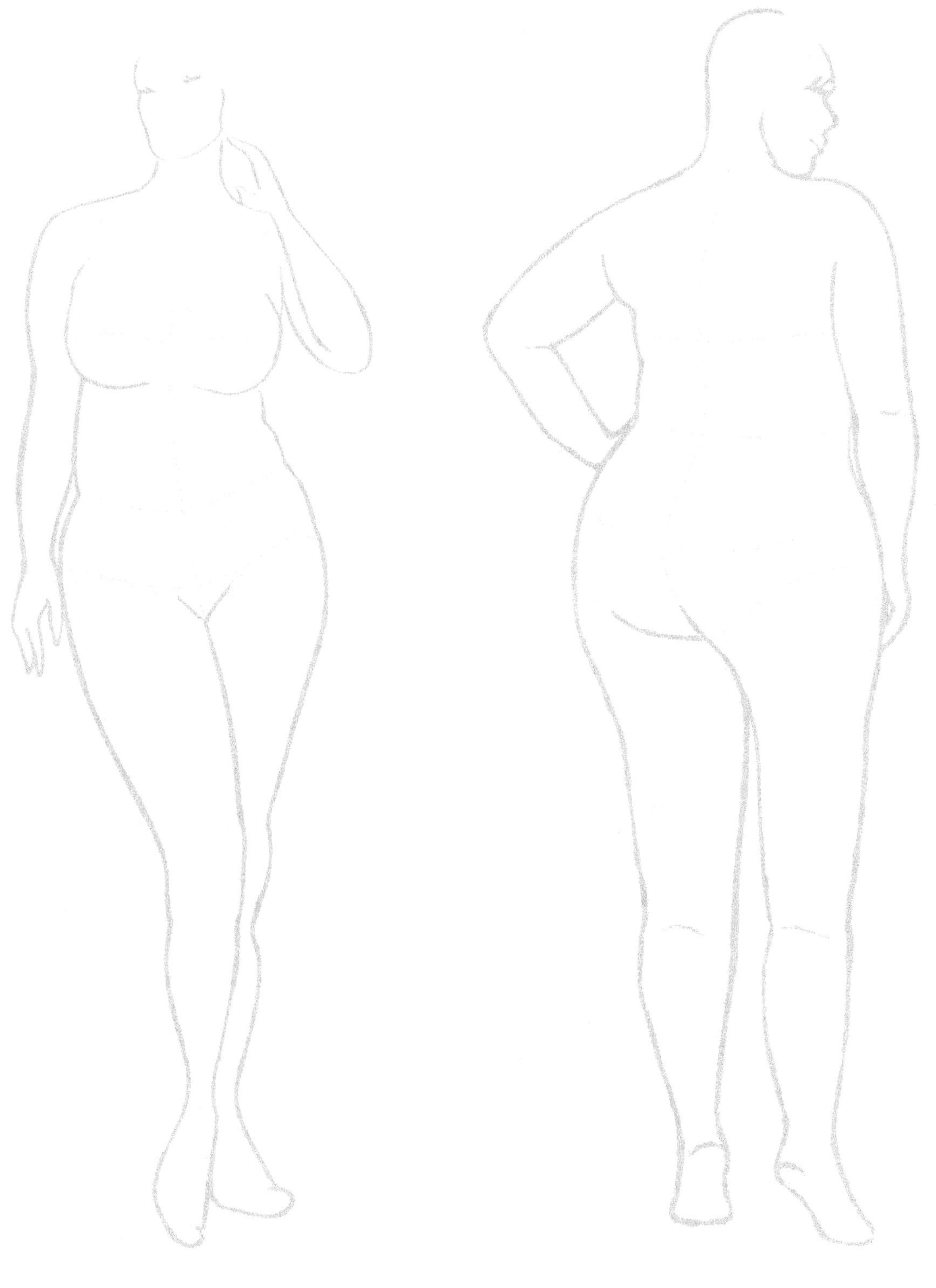

NOTES

NOTES

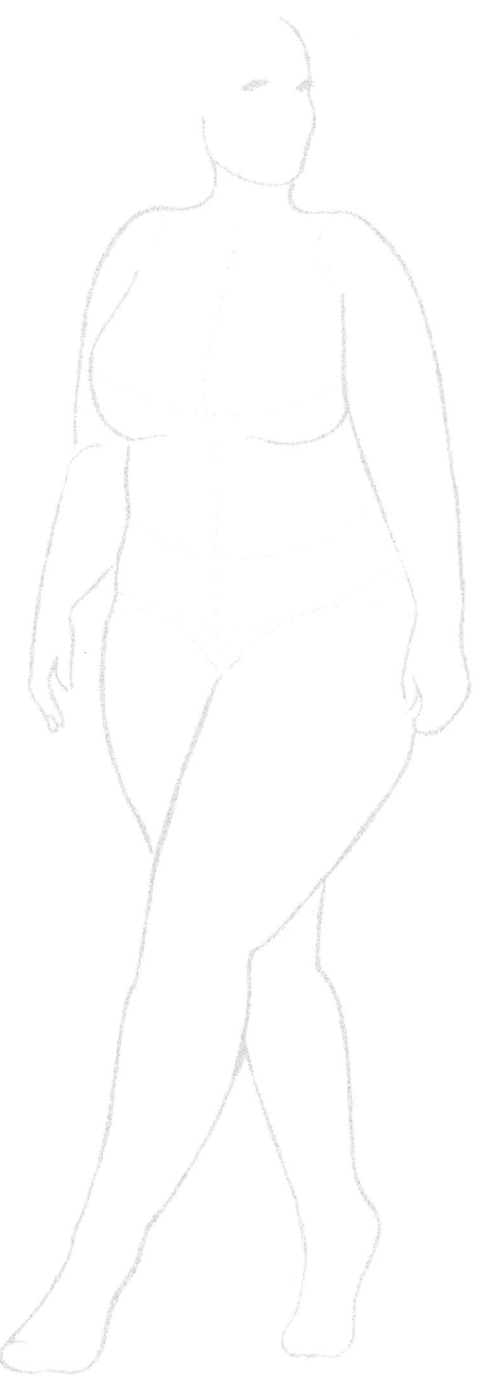

NOTES

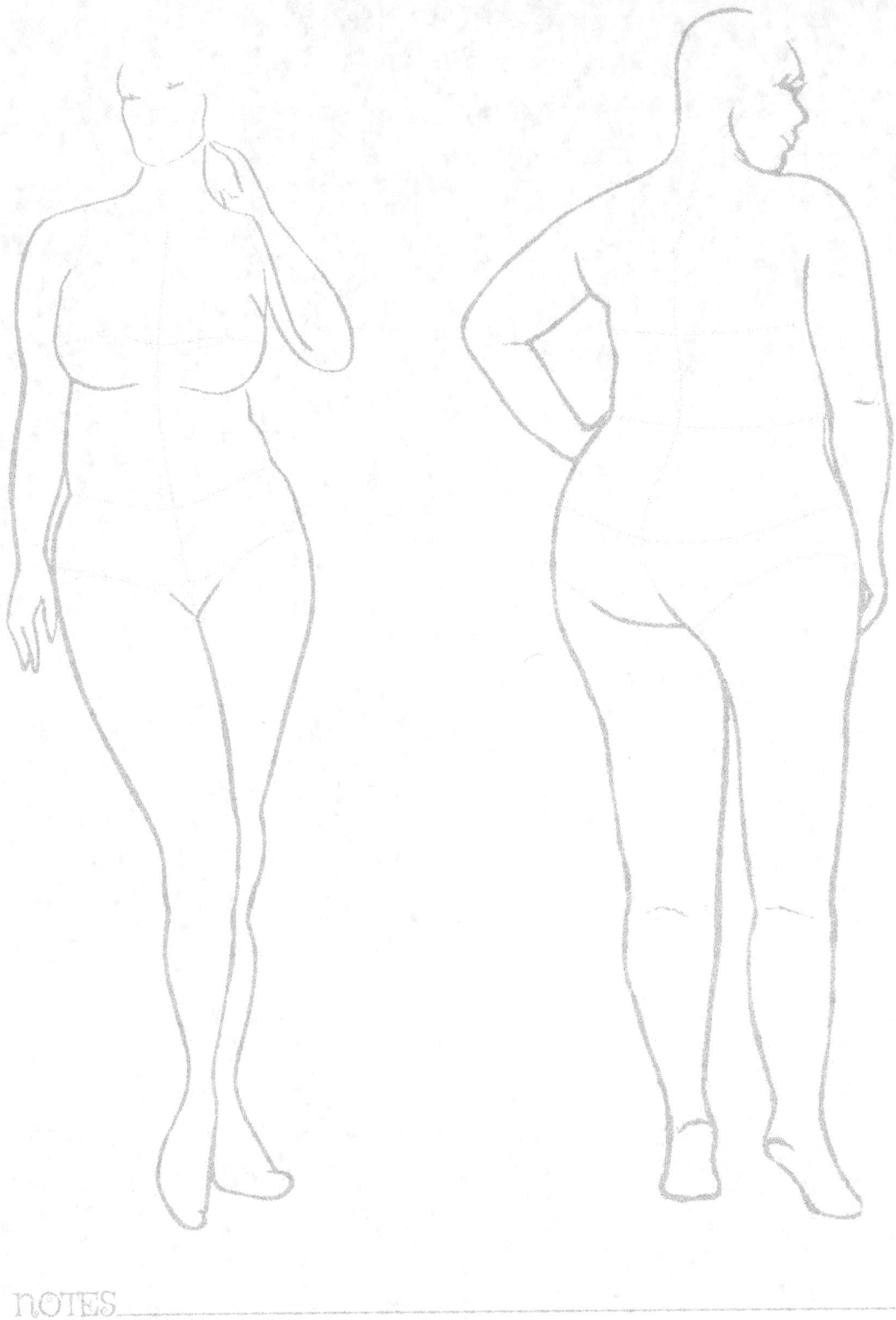

NOTES

NOTES

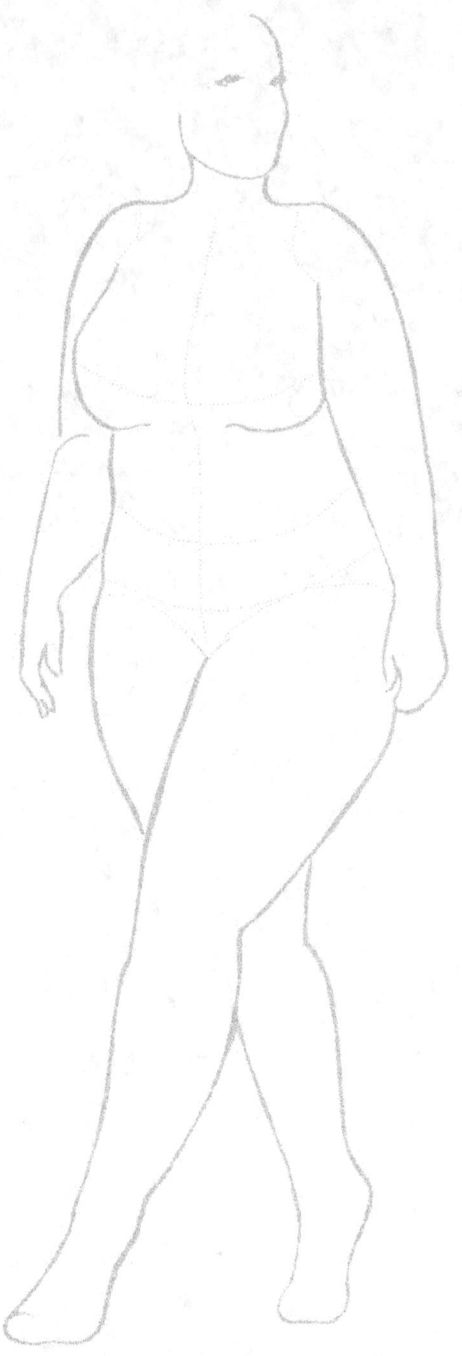

NOTES

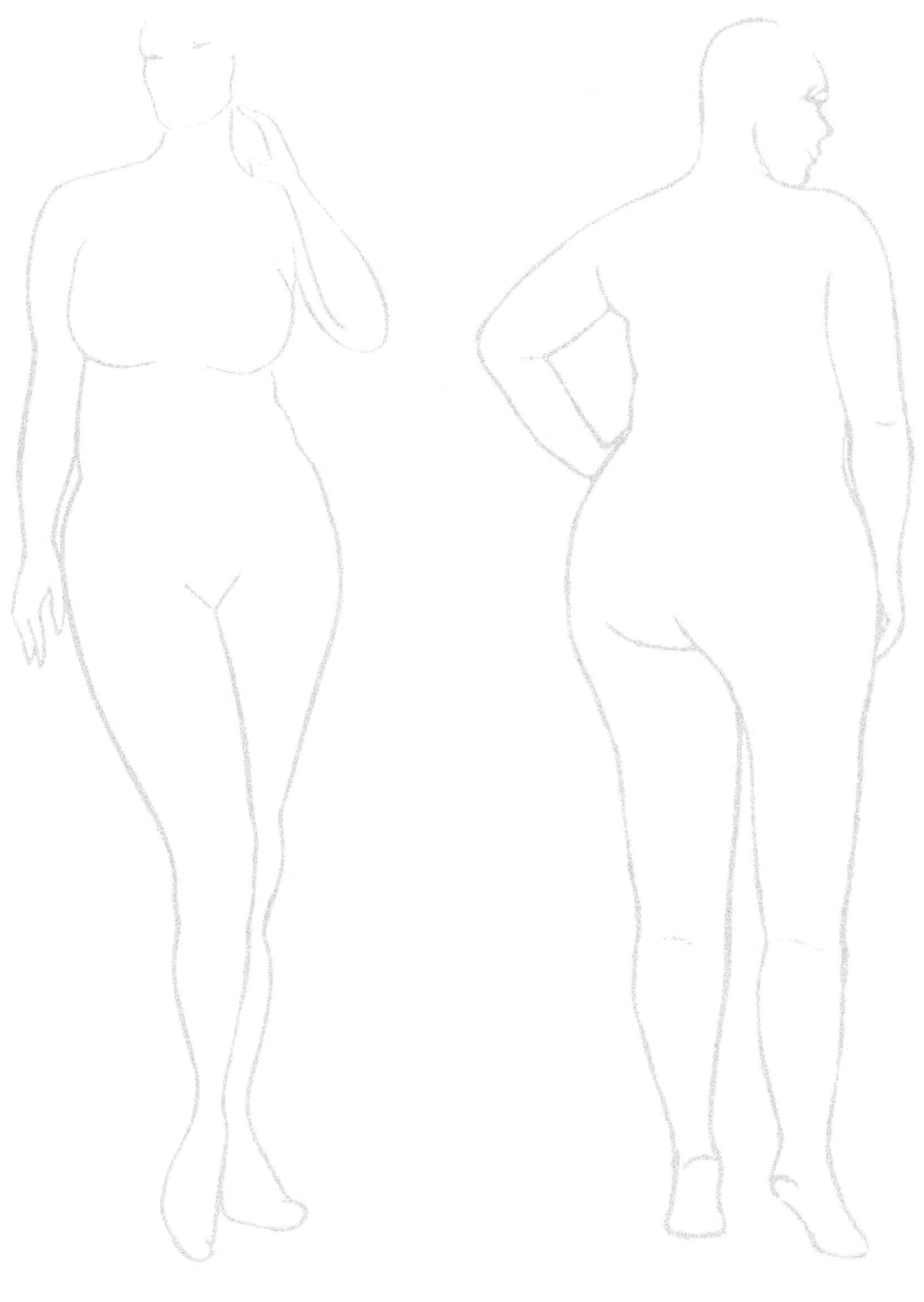

NOTES

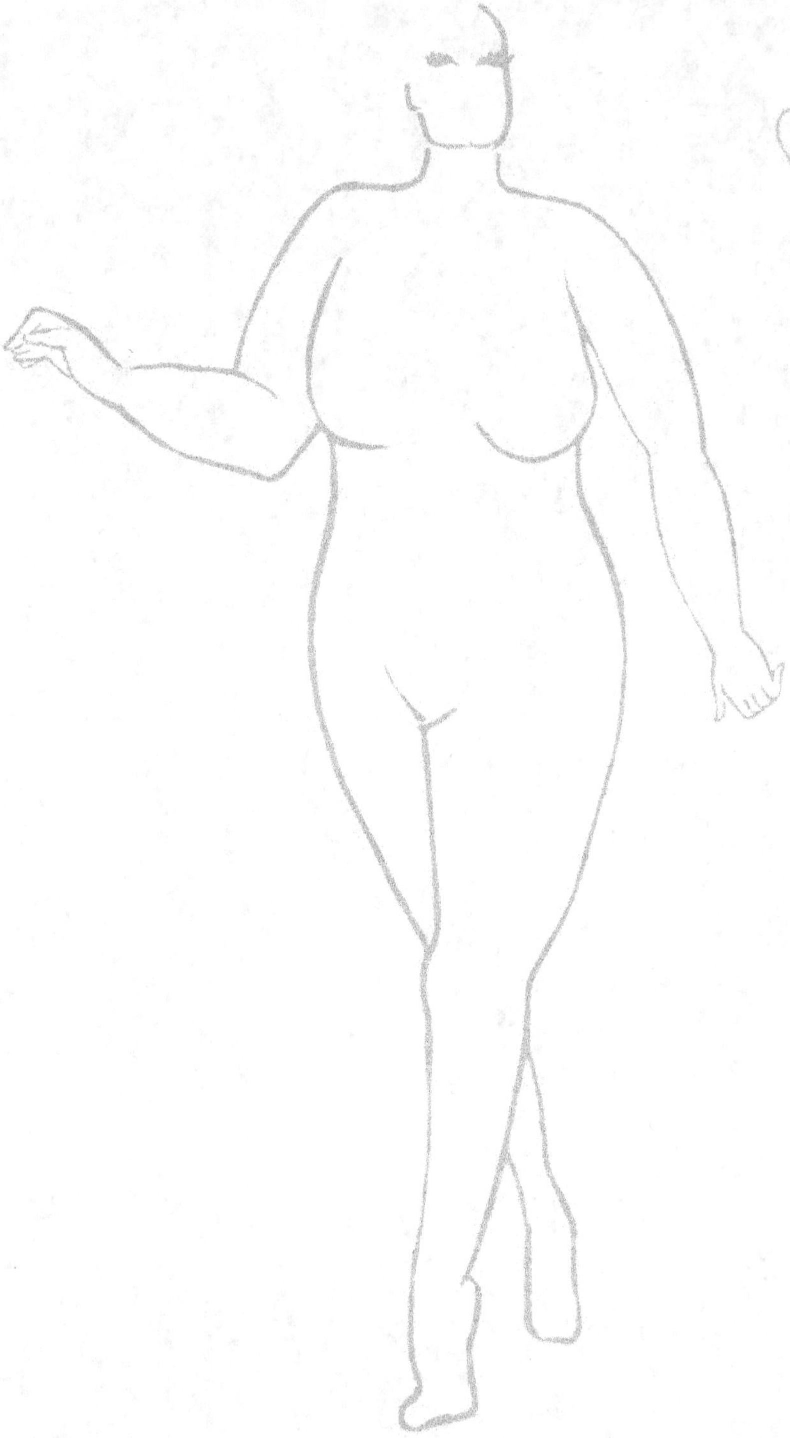

NOTES

NOTES

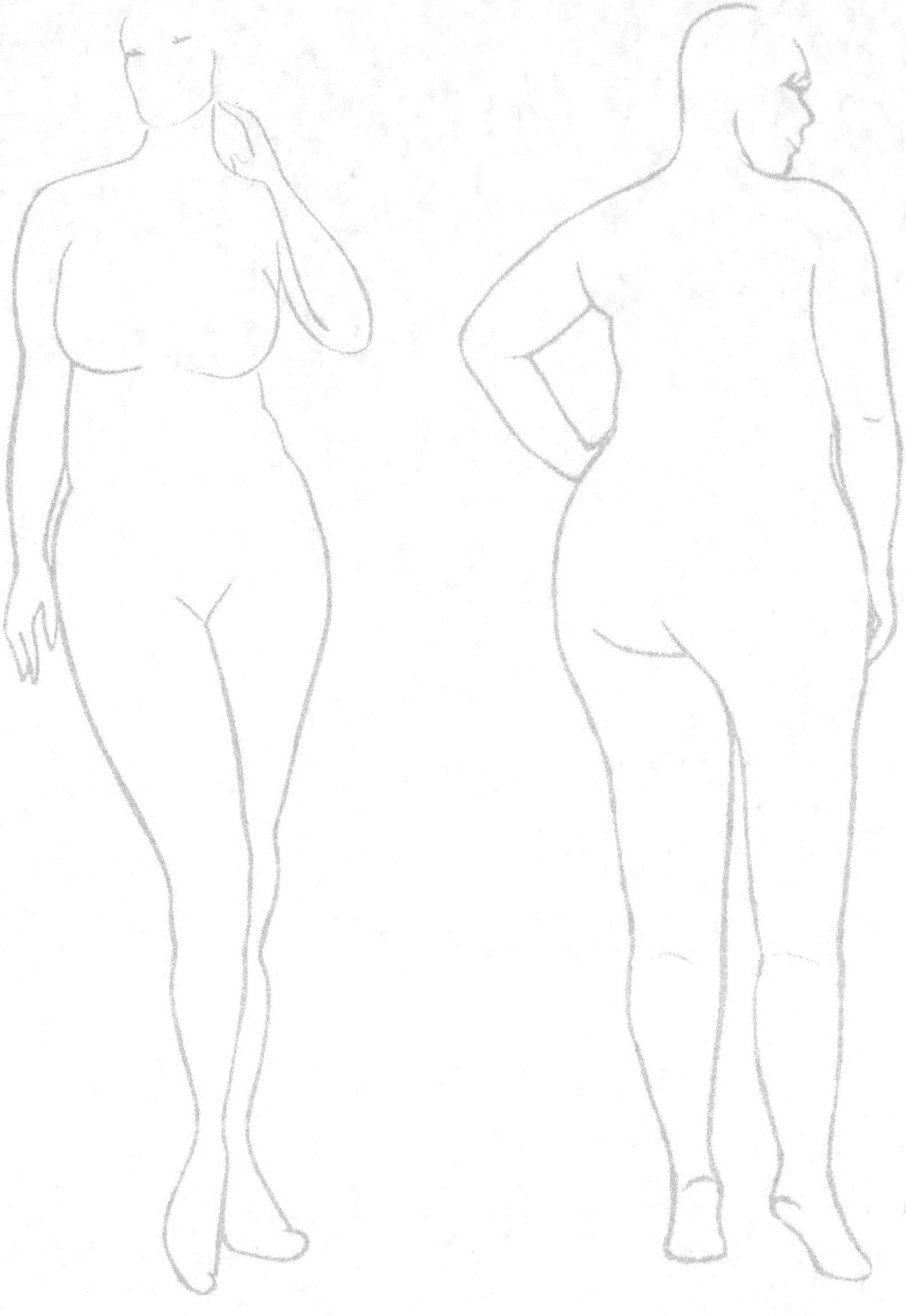

NOTES

NOTES

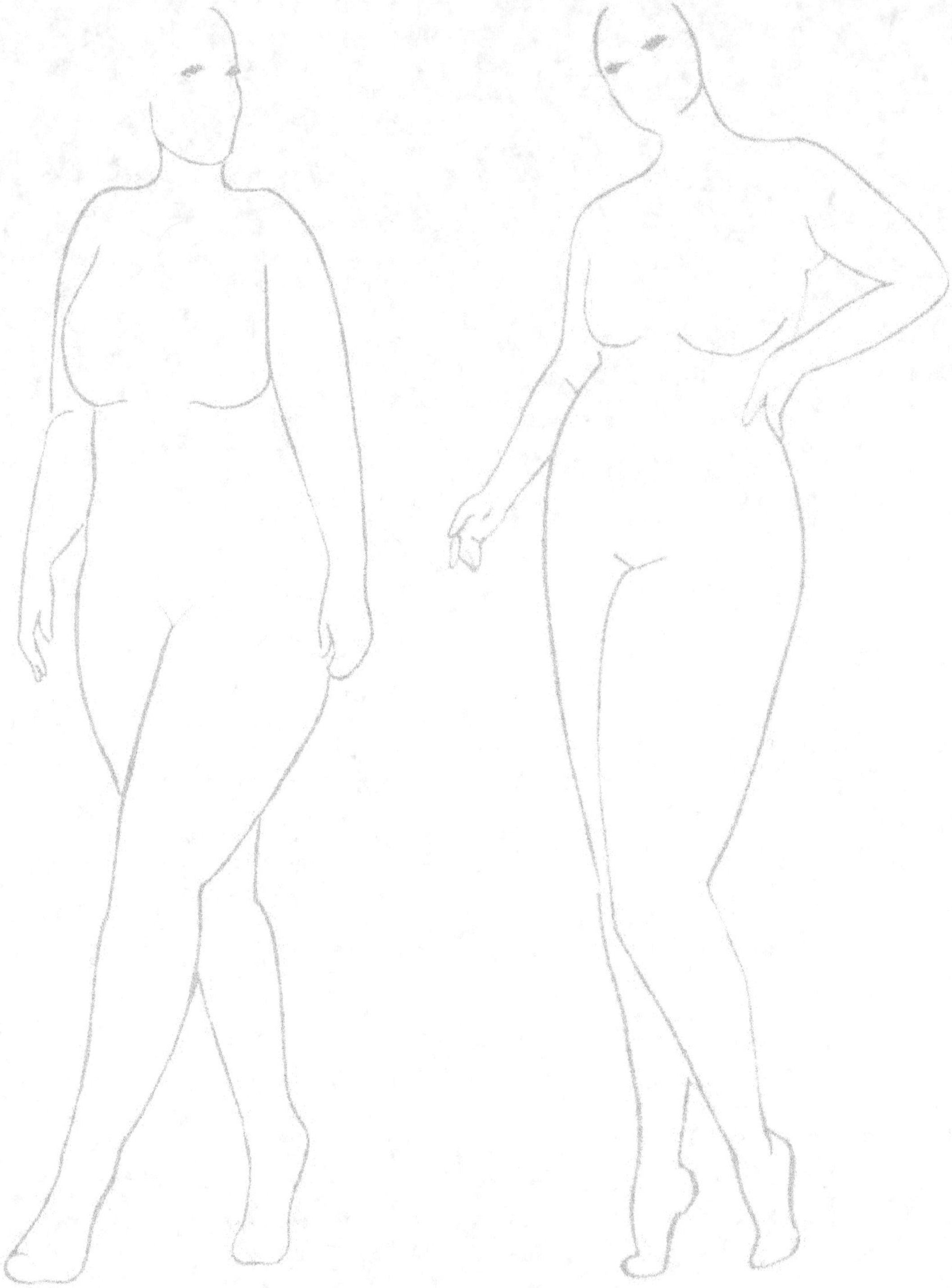

NOTES

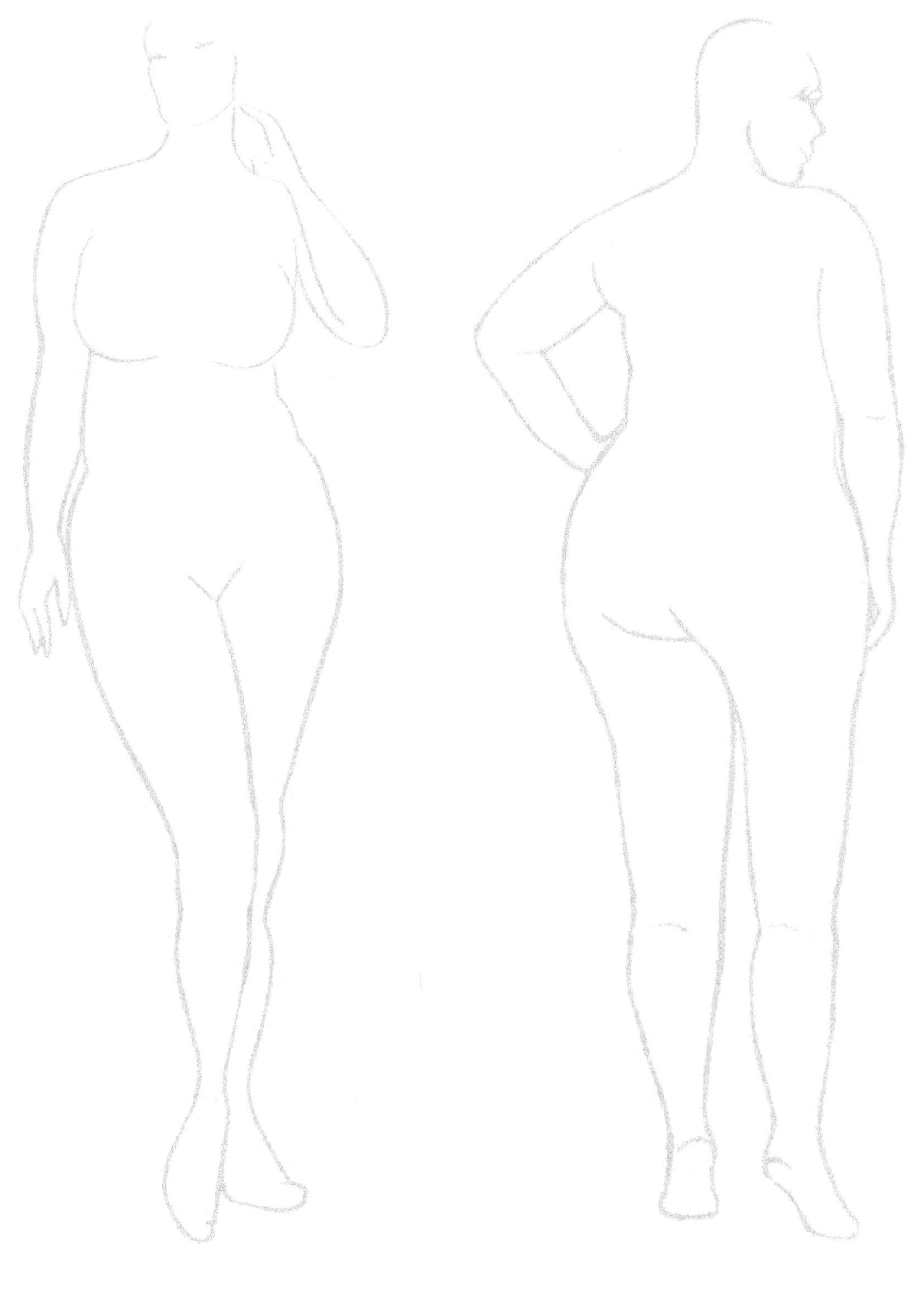

NOTES

NOTES

____

____

____

____

____

NOTES

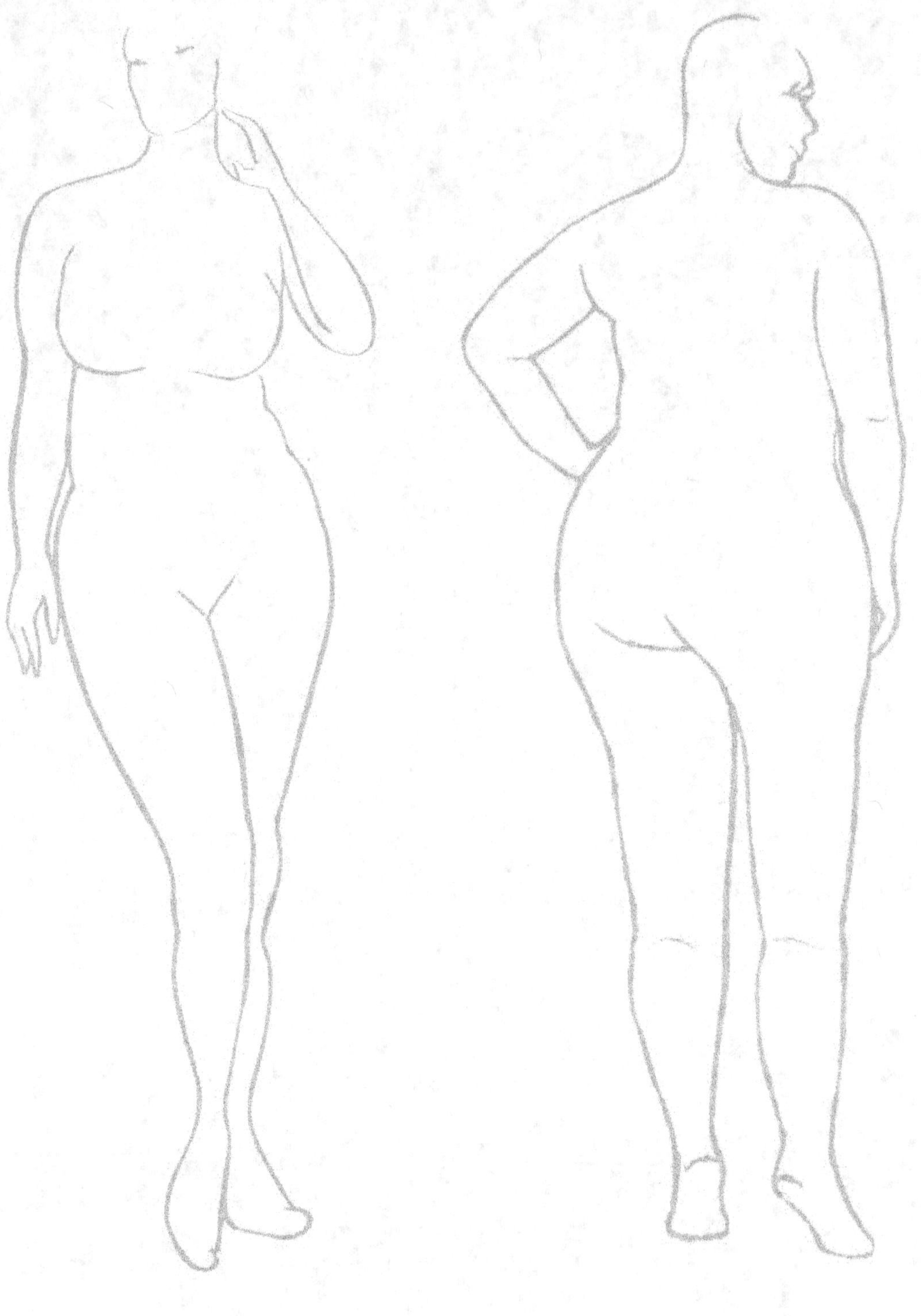

NOTES

NOTES

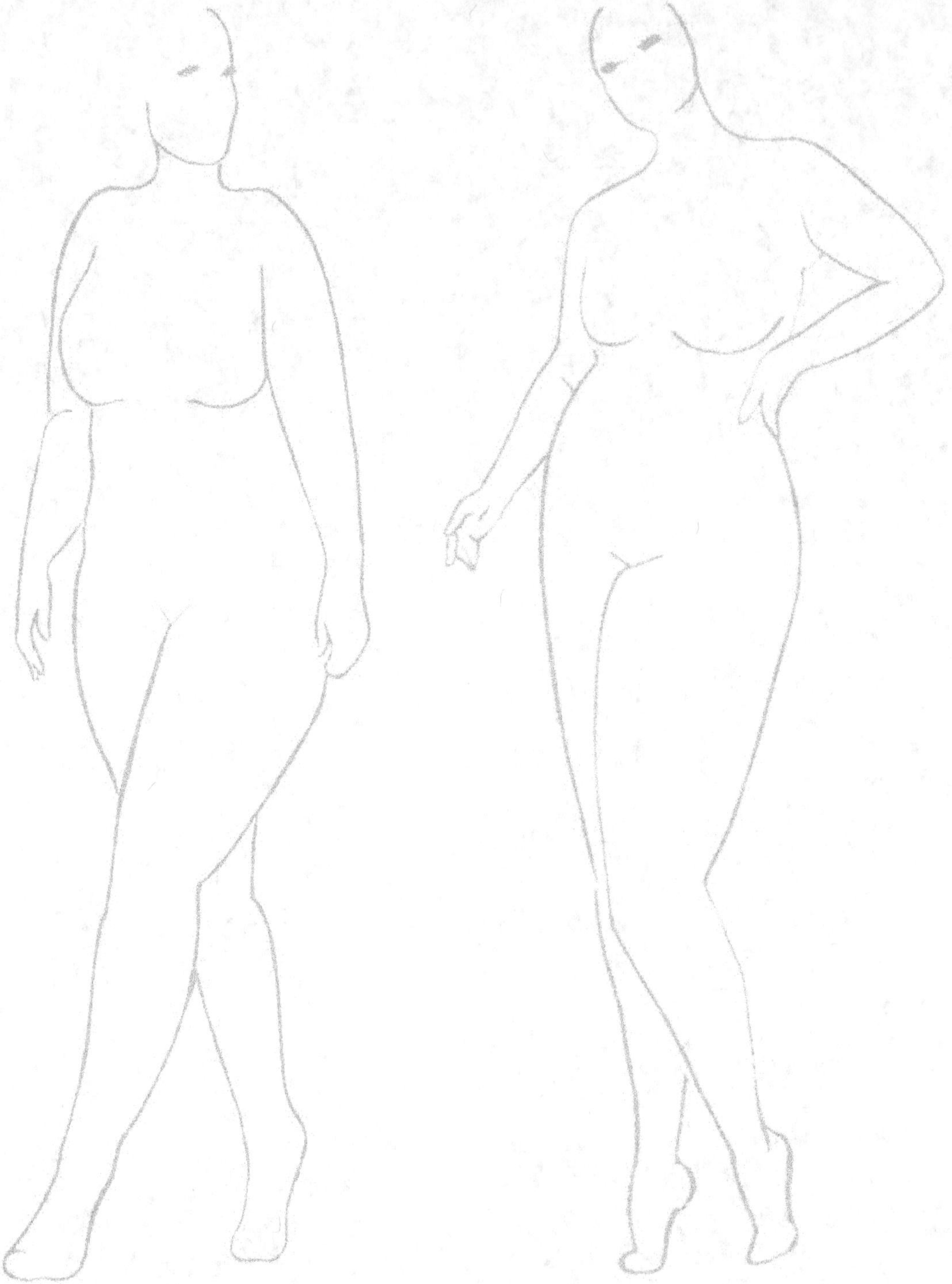

NOTES

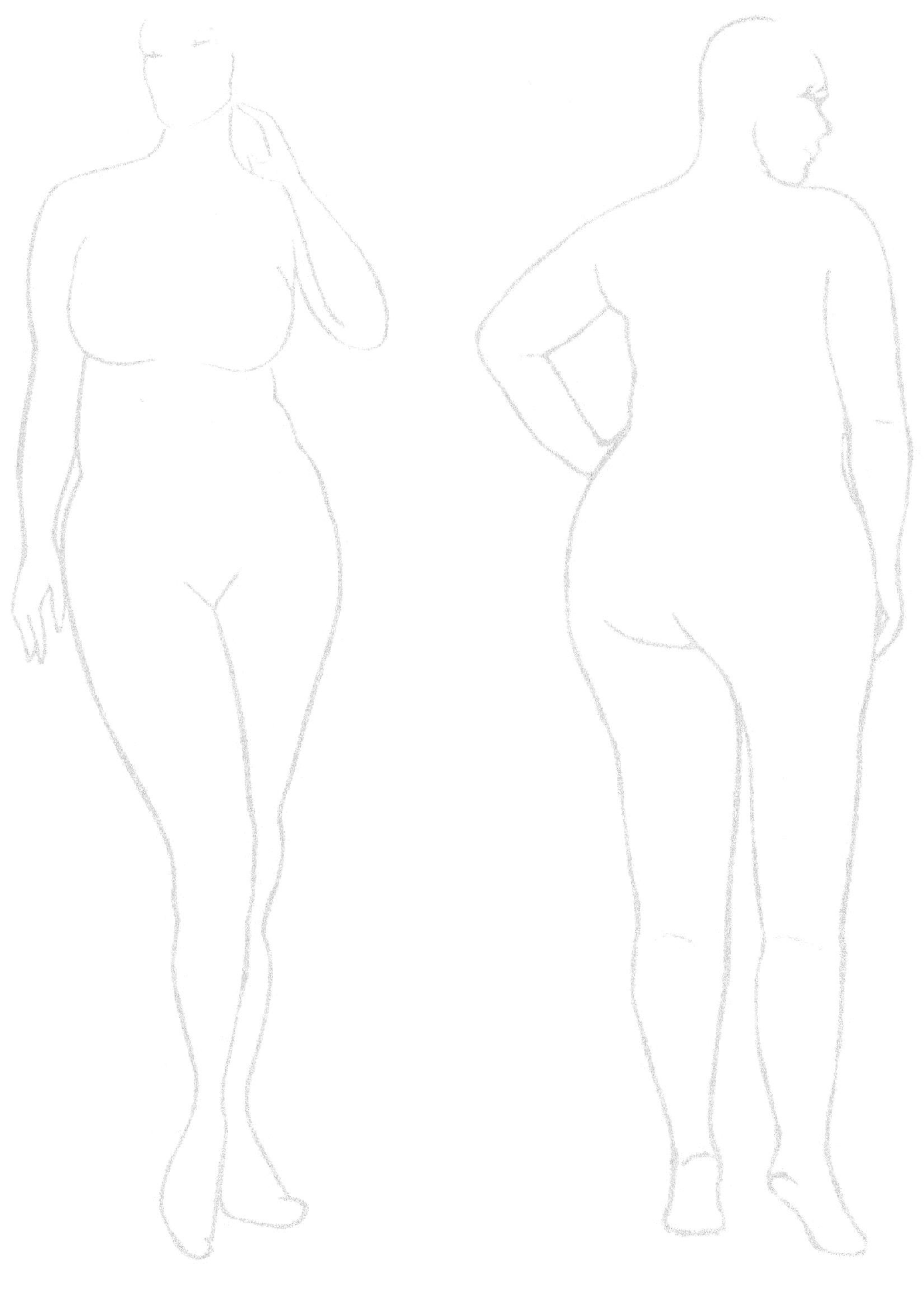

NOTES

NOTES

NOTES

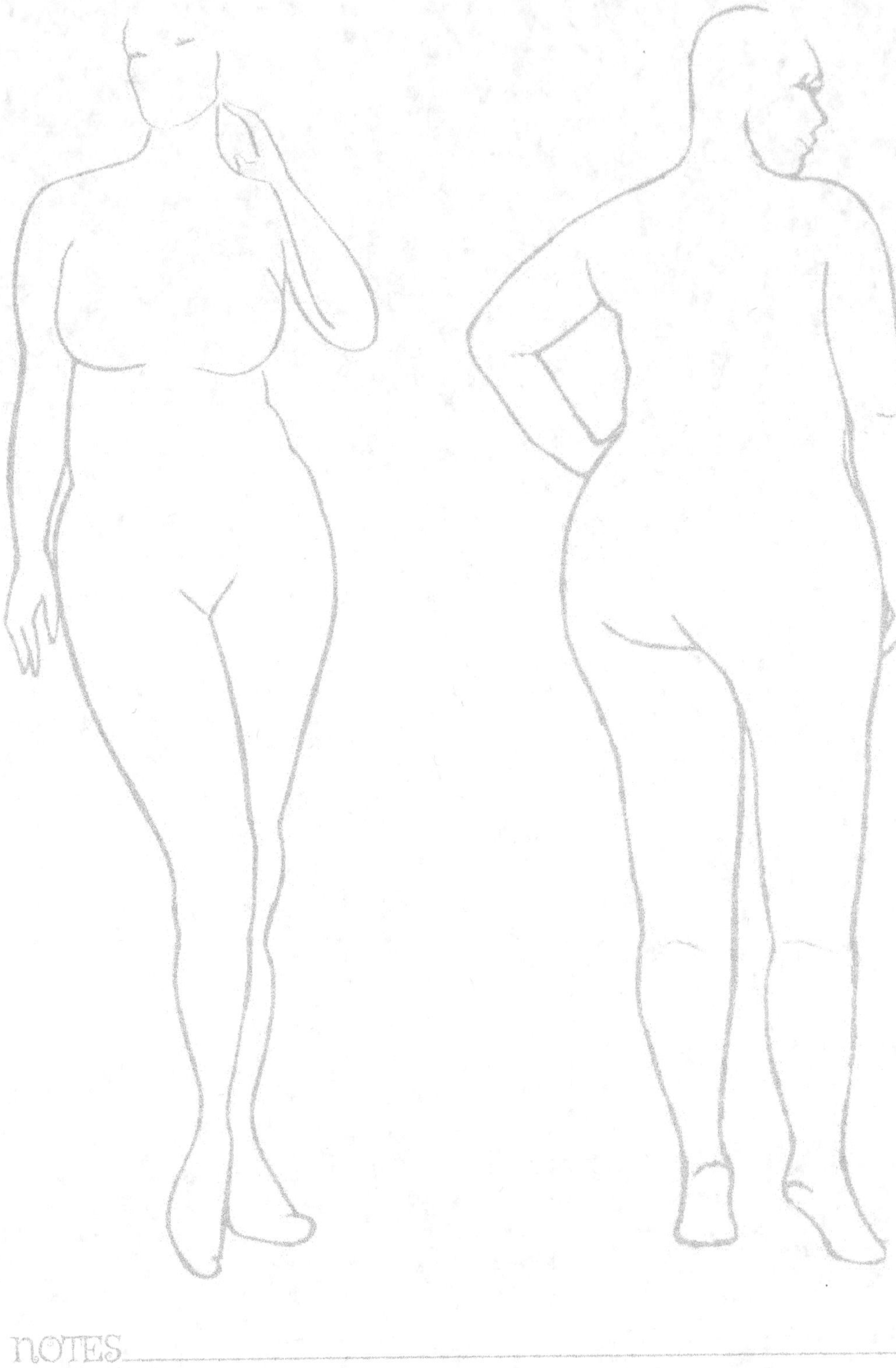

NOTES

NOTES

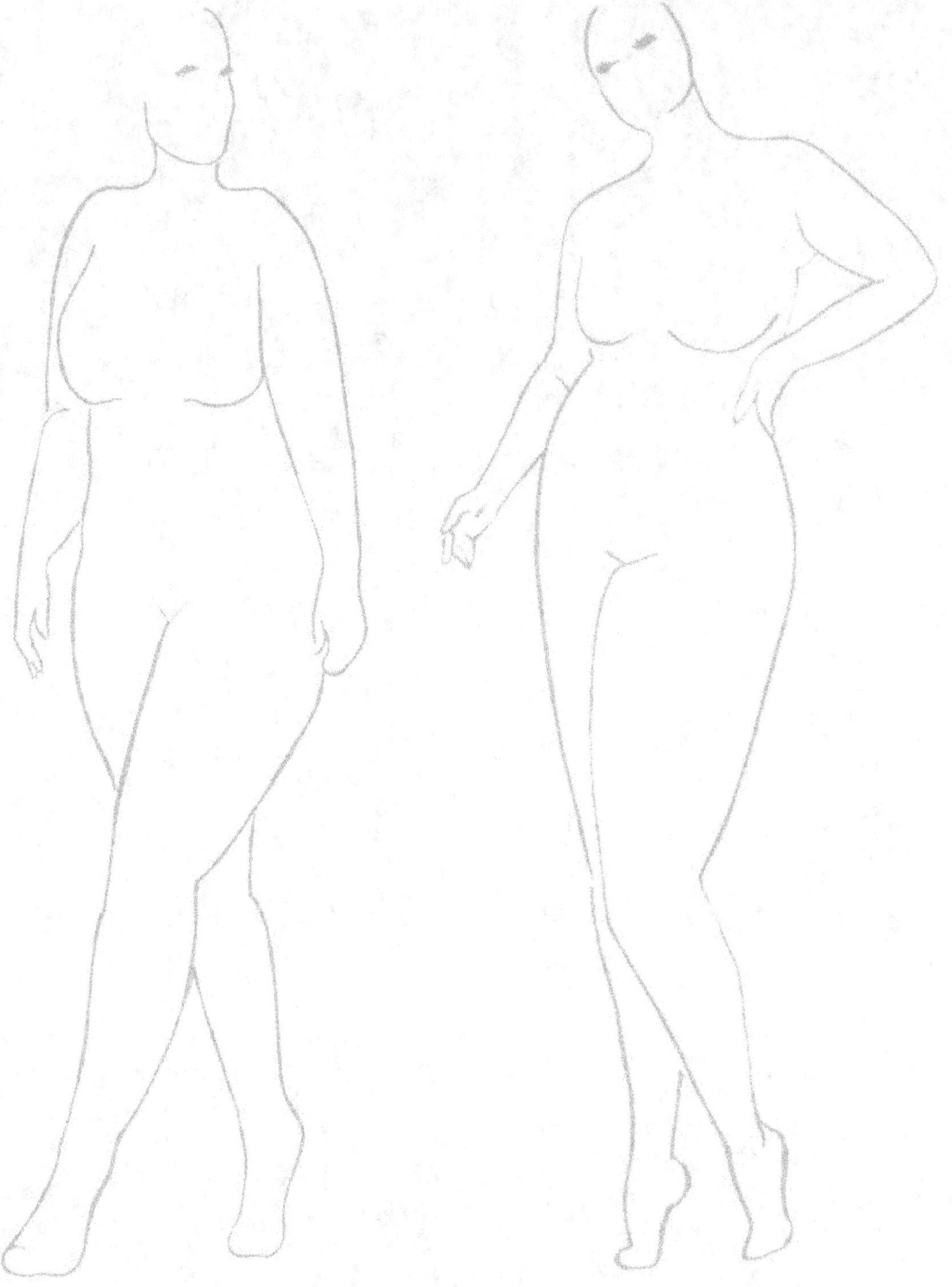

NOTES

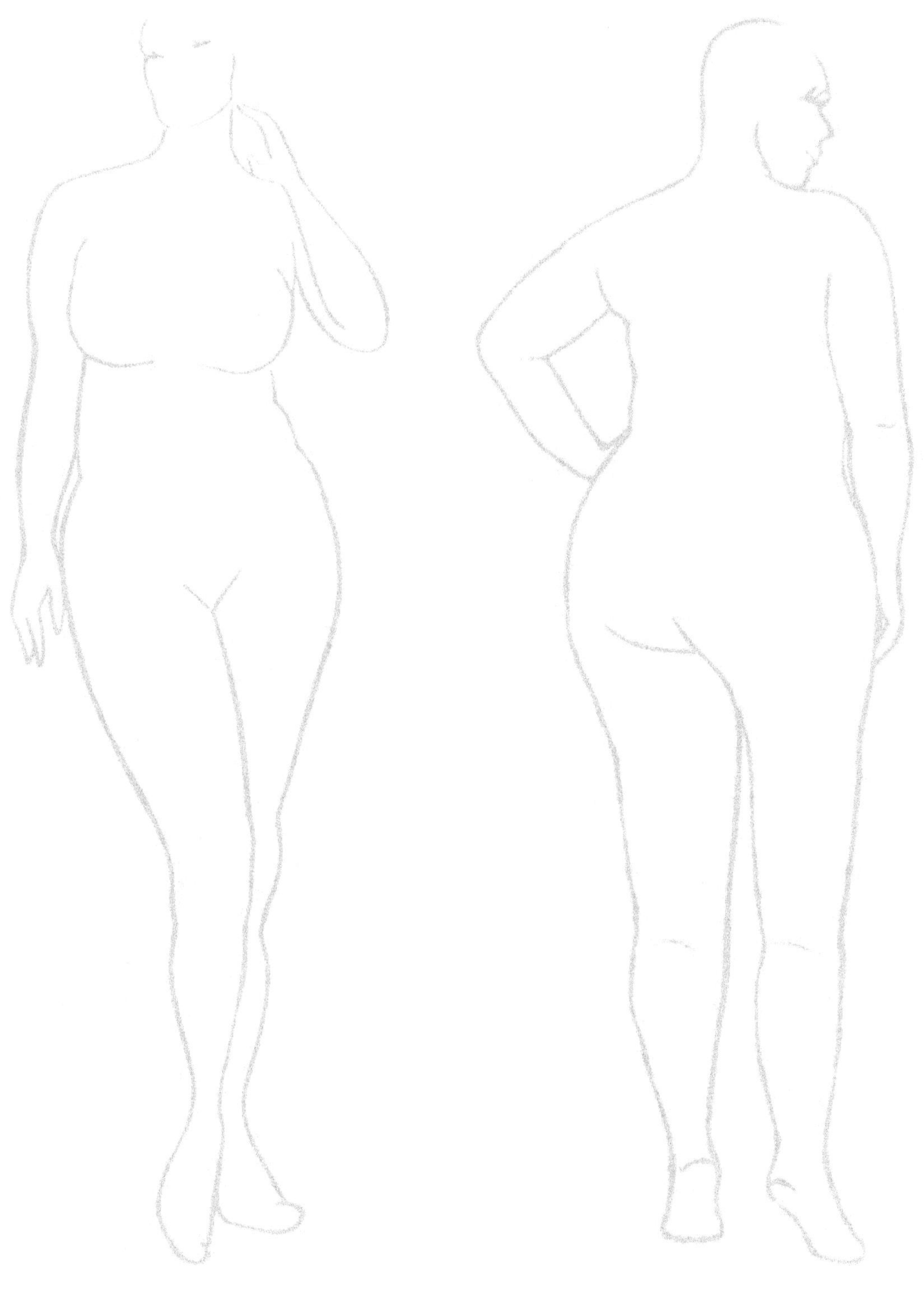

NOTES

NOTES

NOTES

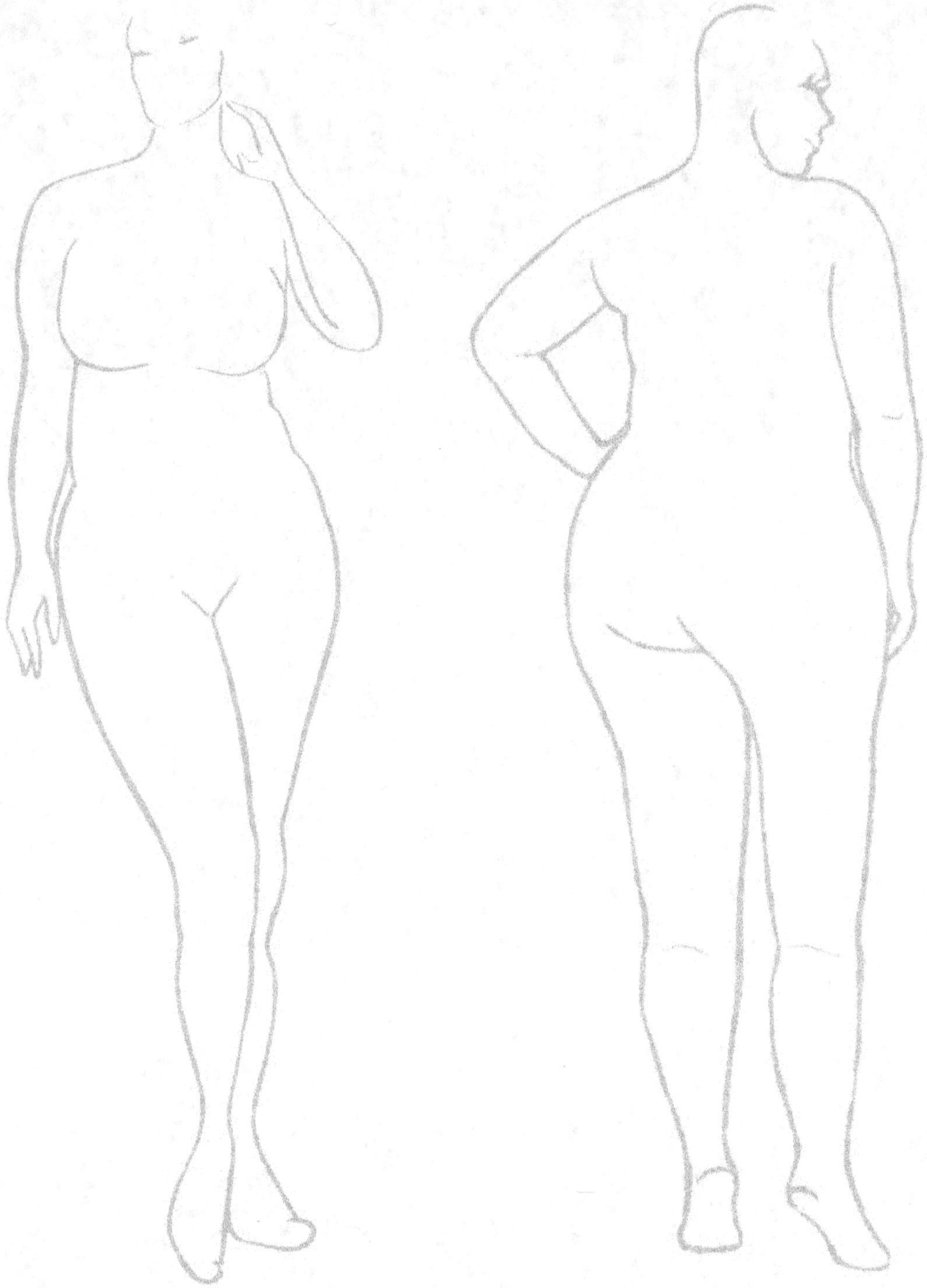

NOTES

____

____

____

____

____

NOTES

NOTES

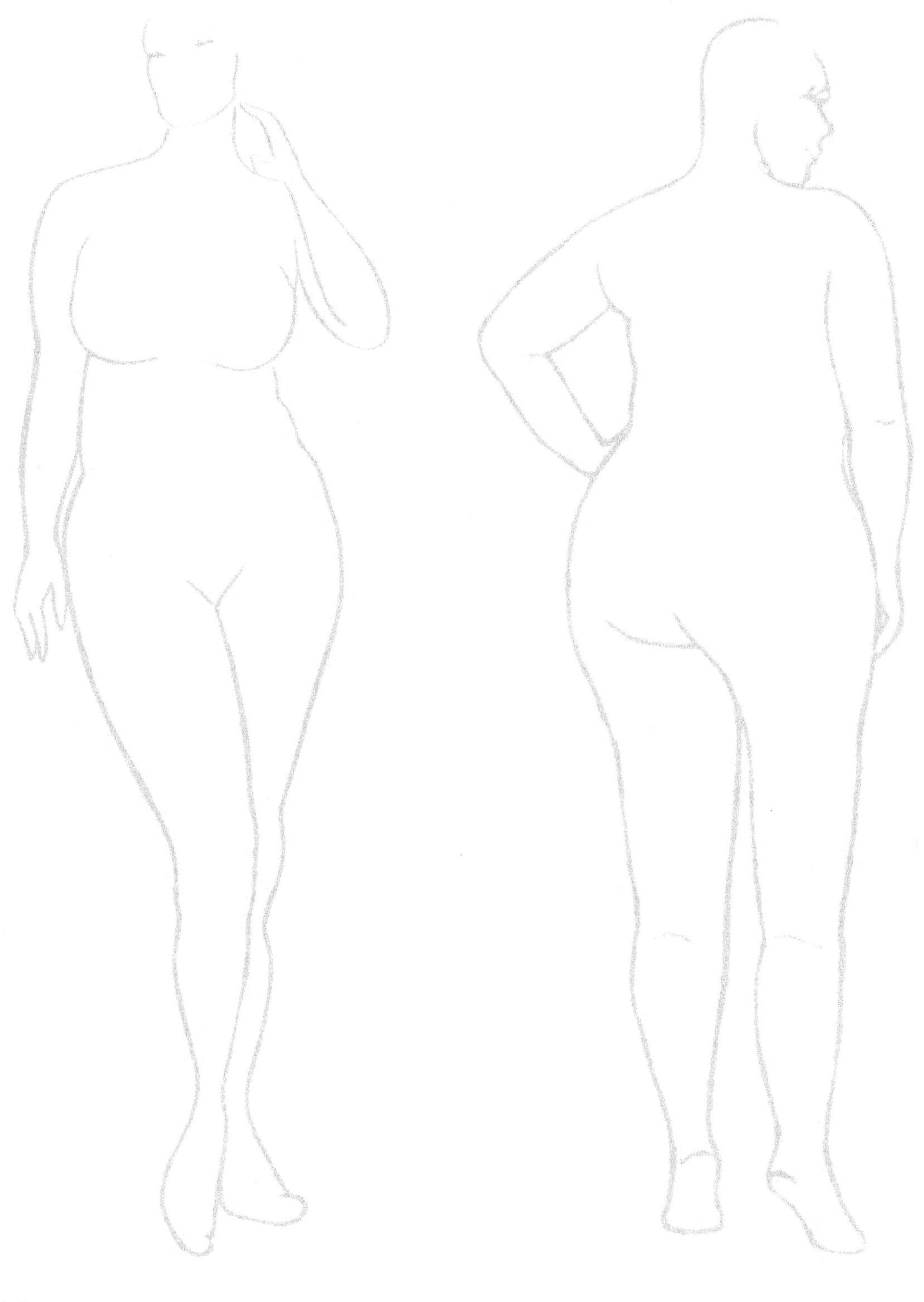

NOTES

NOTES____
____
____
____
____
____

NOTES

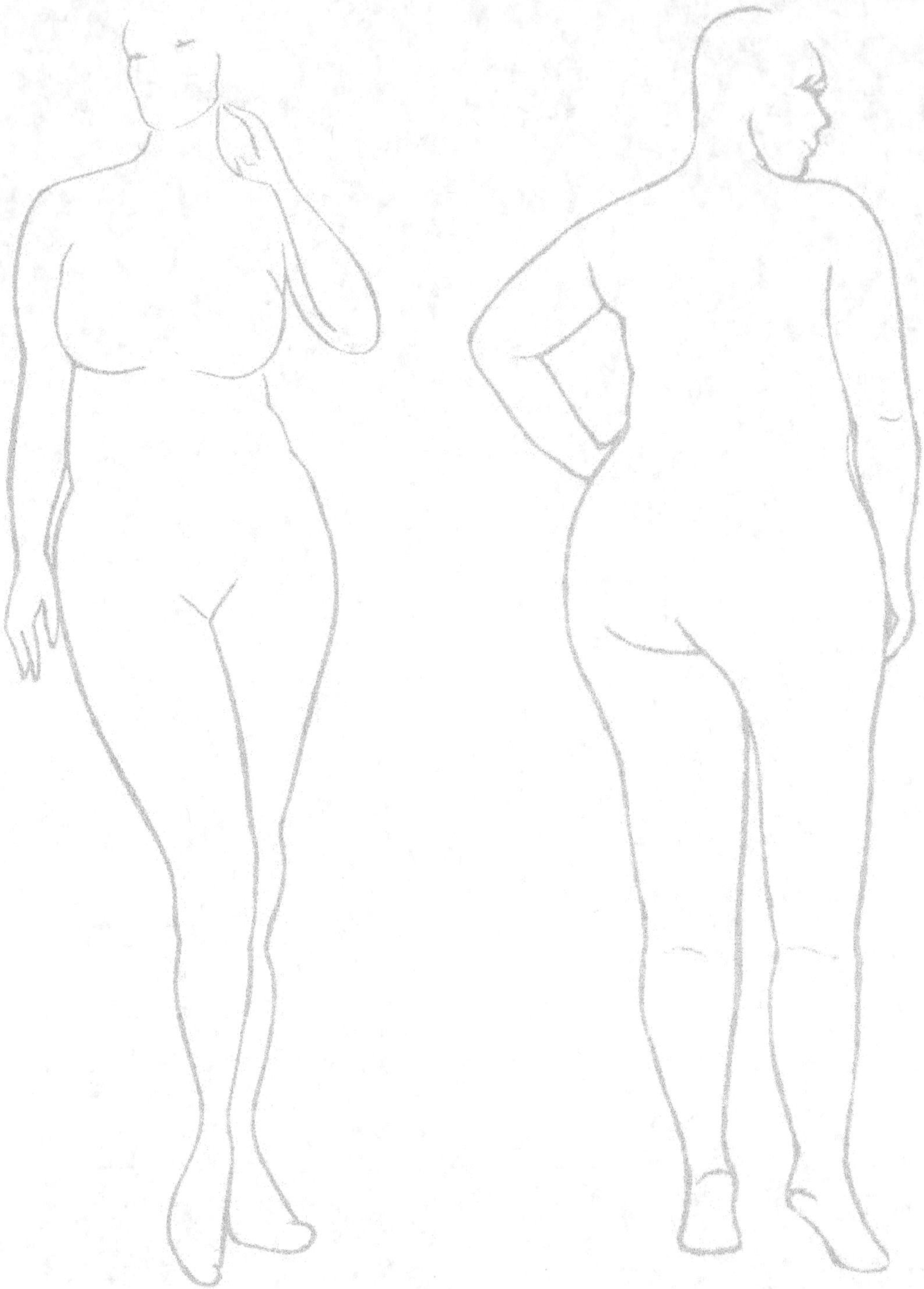

NOTES____

____

____

____

____

____

NOTES

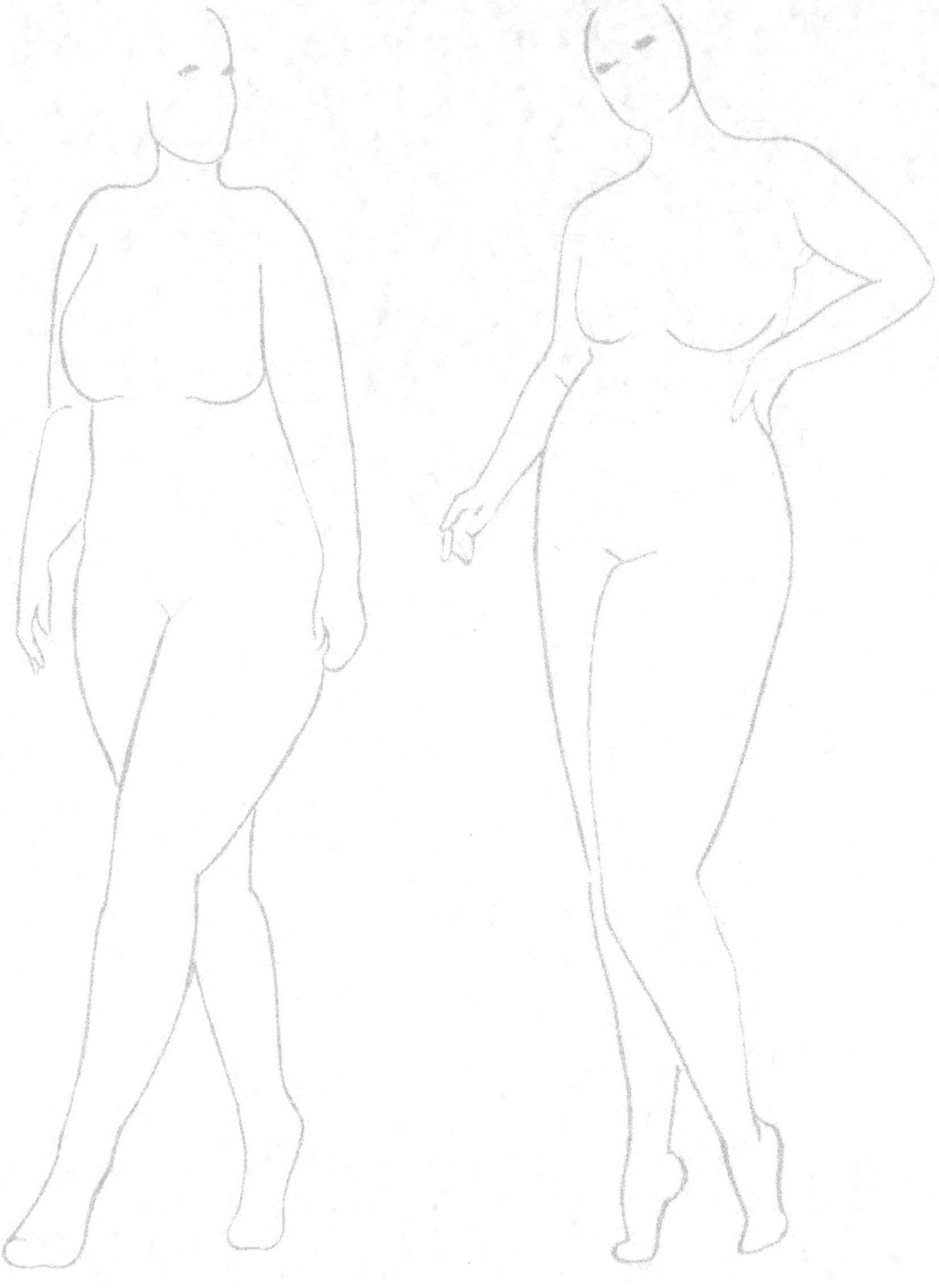

NOTES

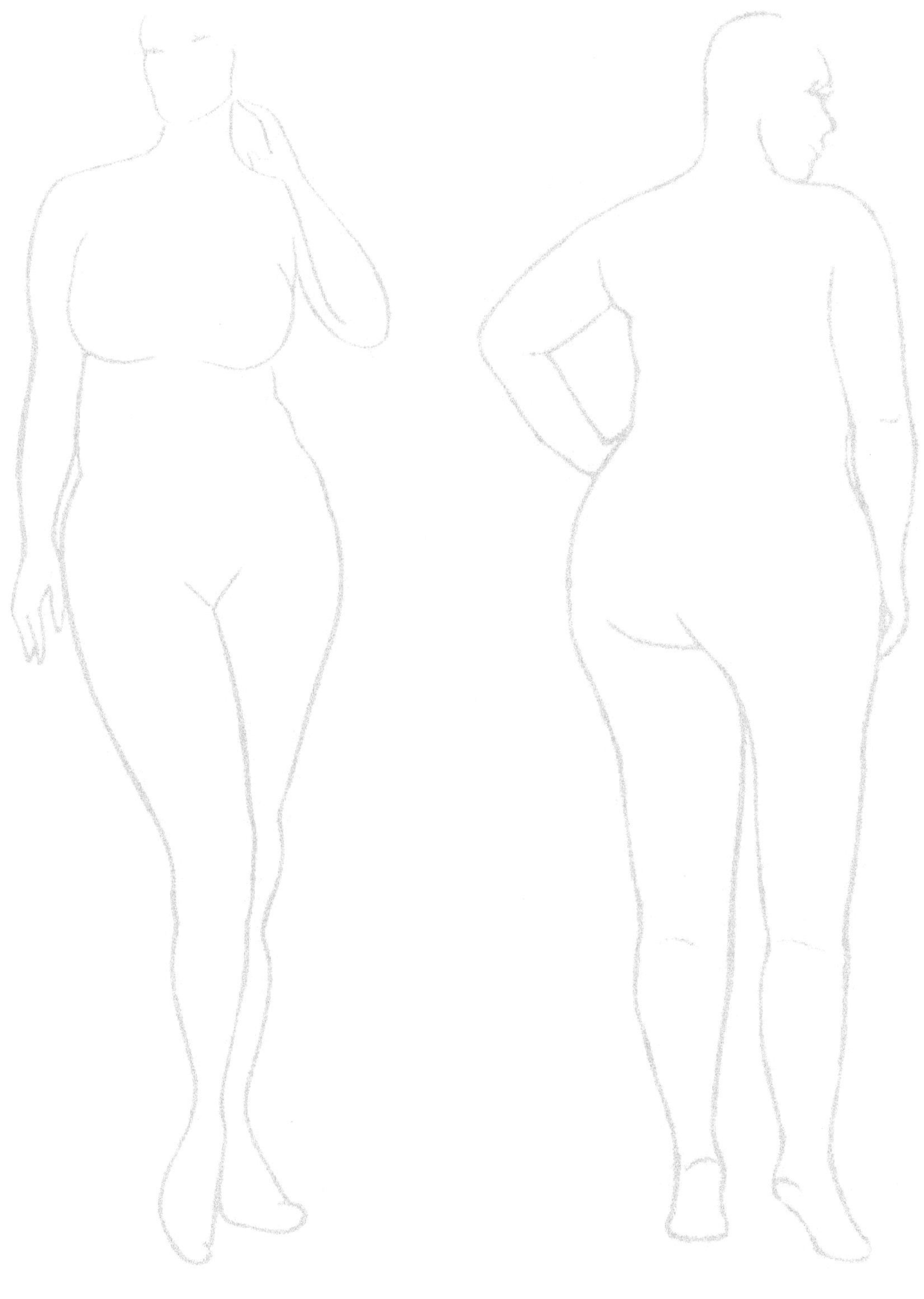

NOTES

NOTES

NOTES

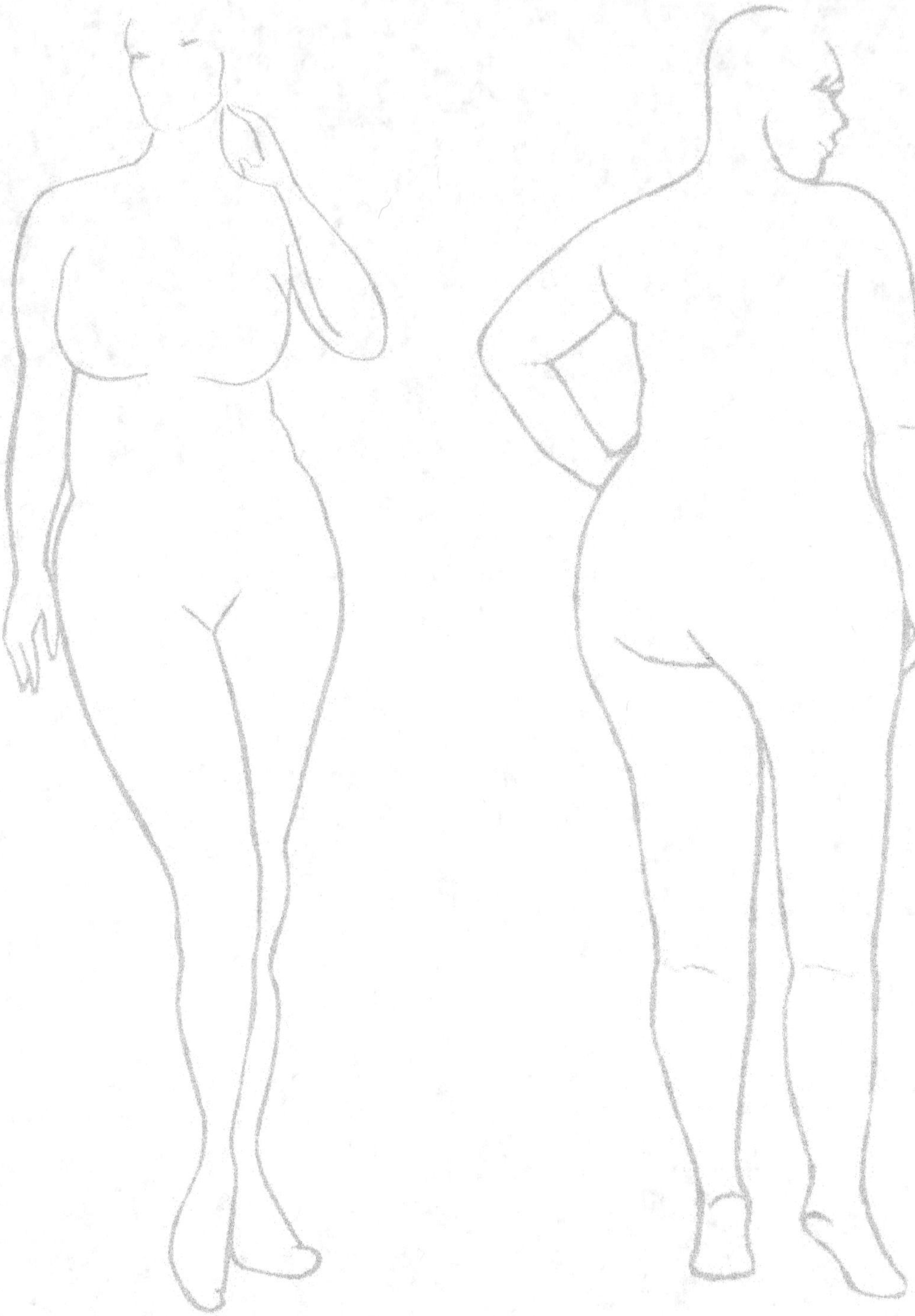

NOTES

NOTES

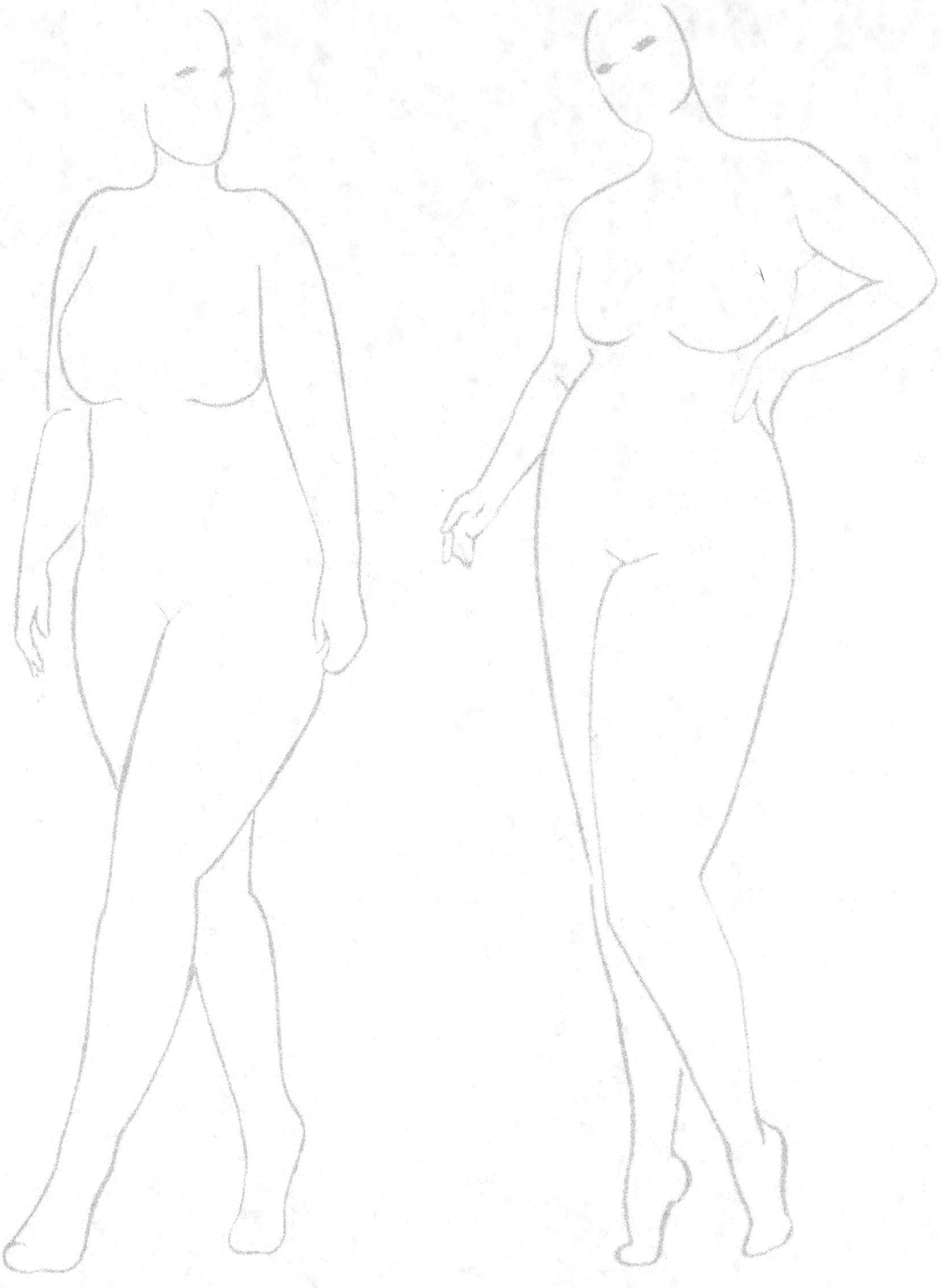

NOTES____

____

____

____

____

____

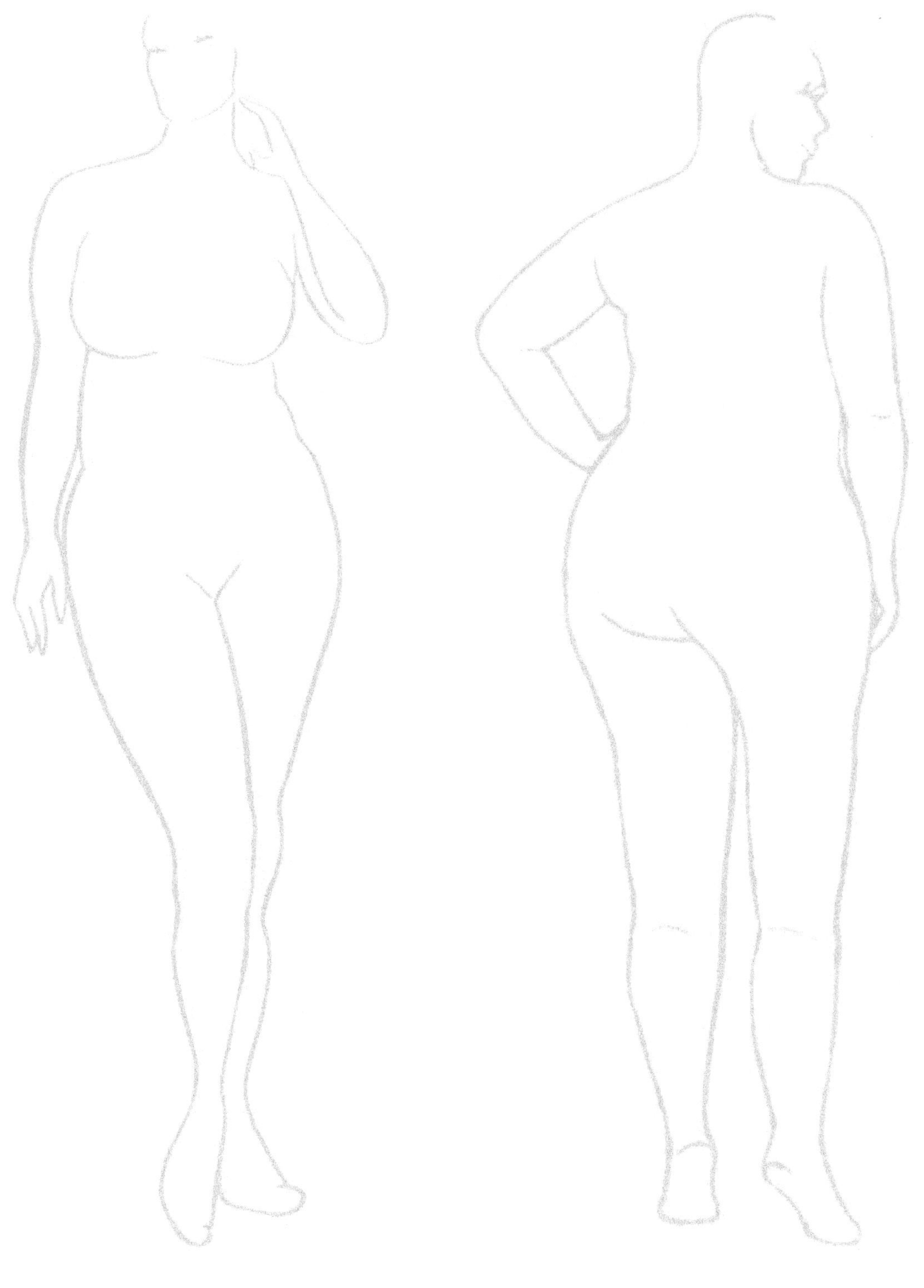

NOTES

NOTES

NOTES

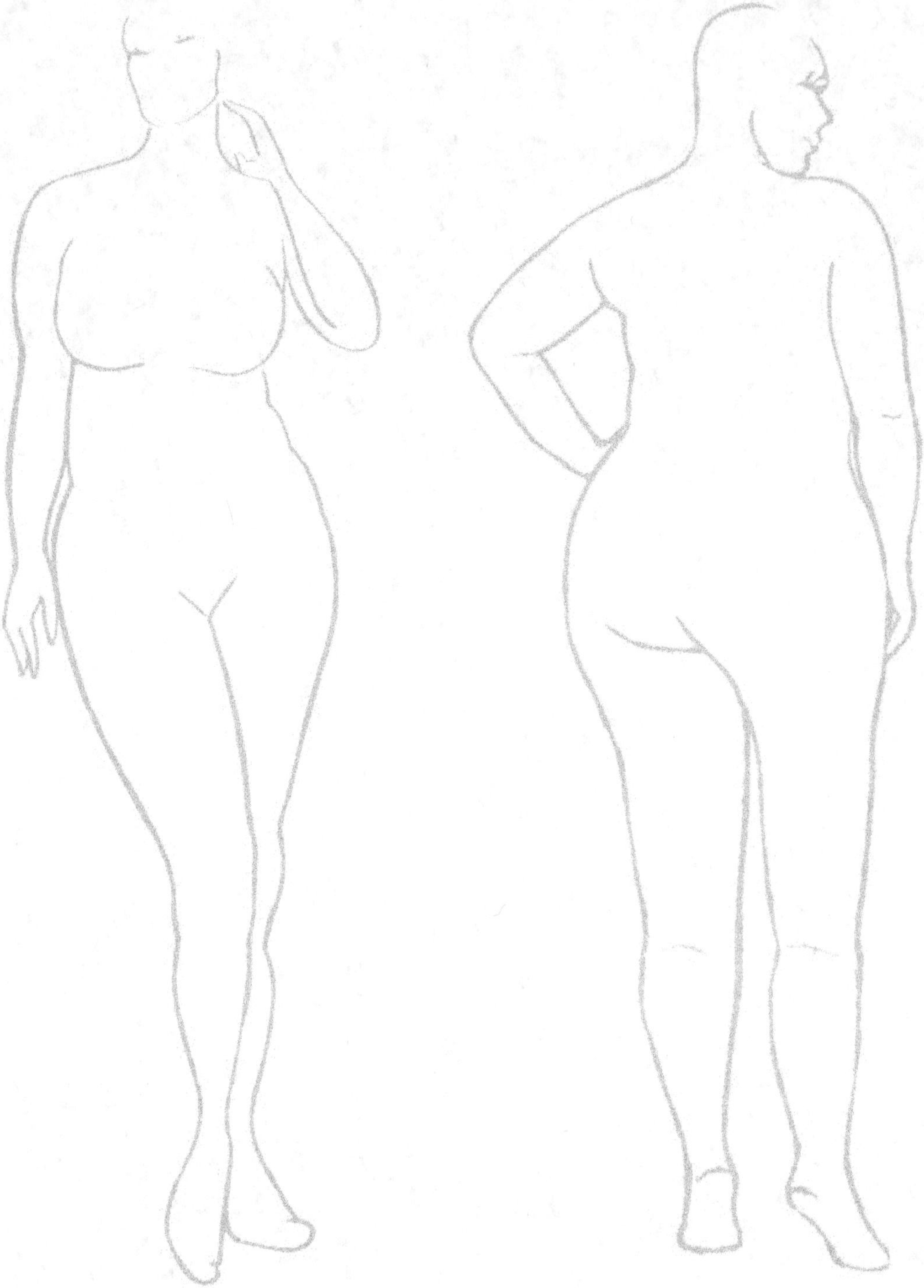

NOTES____

____

____

____

____

____

NOTES

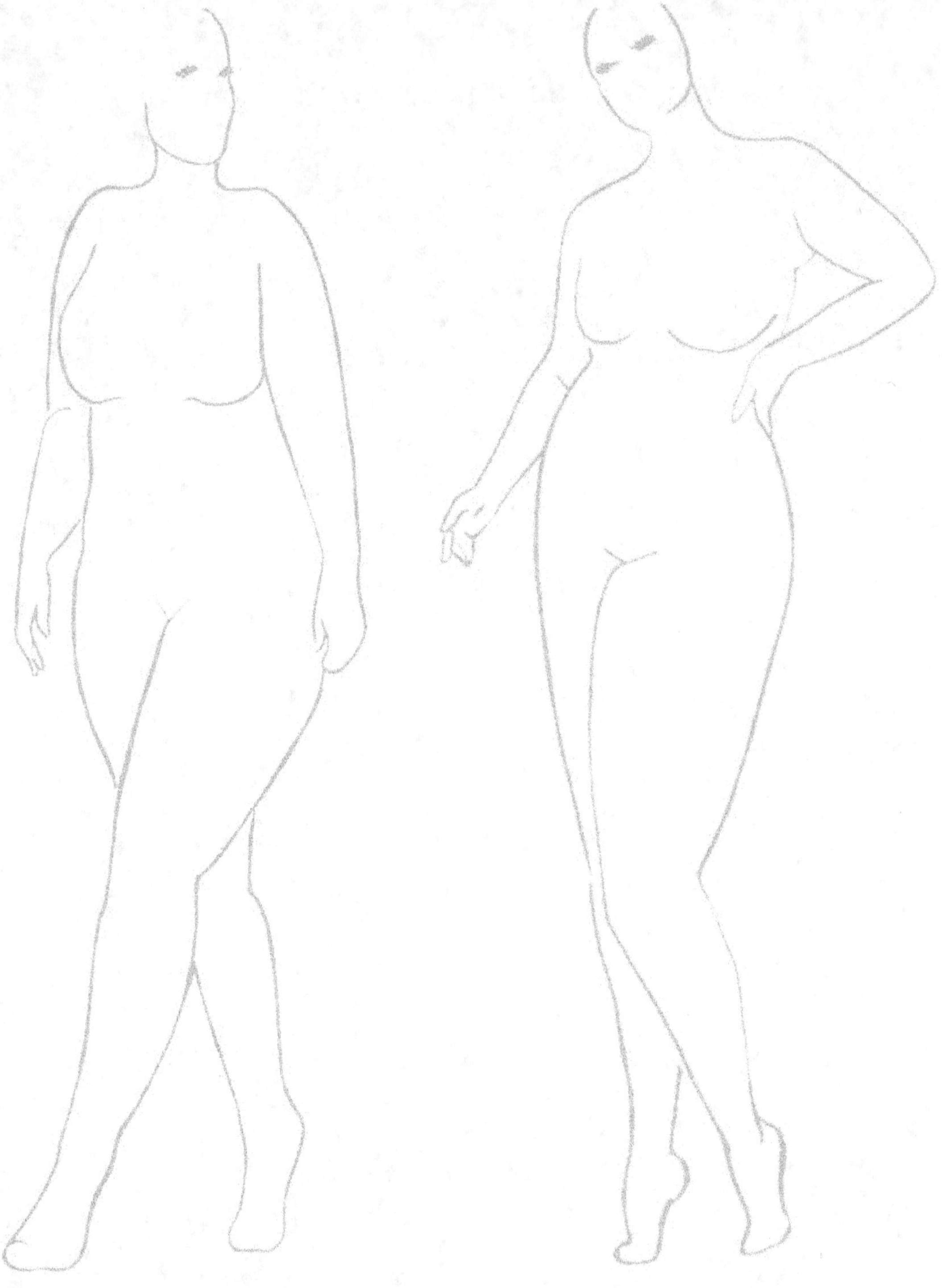

NOTES

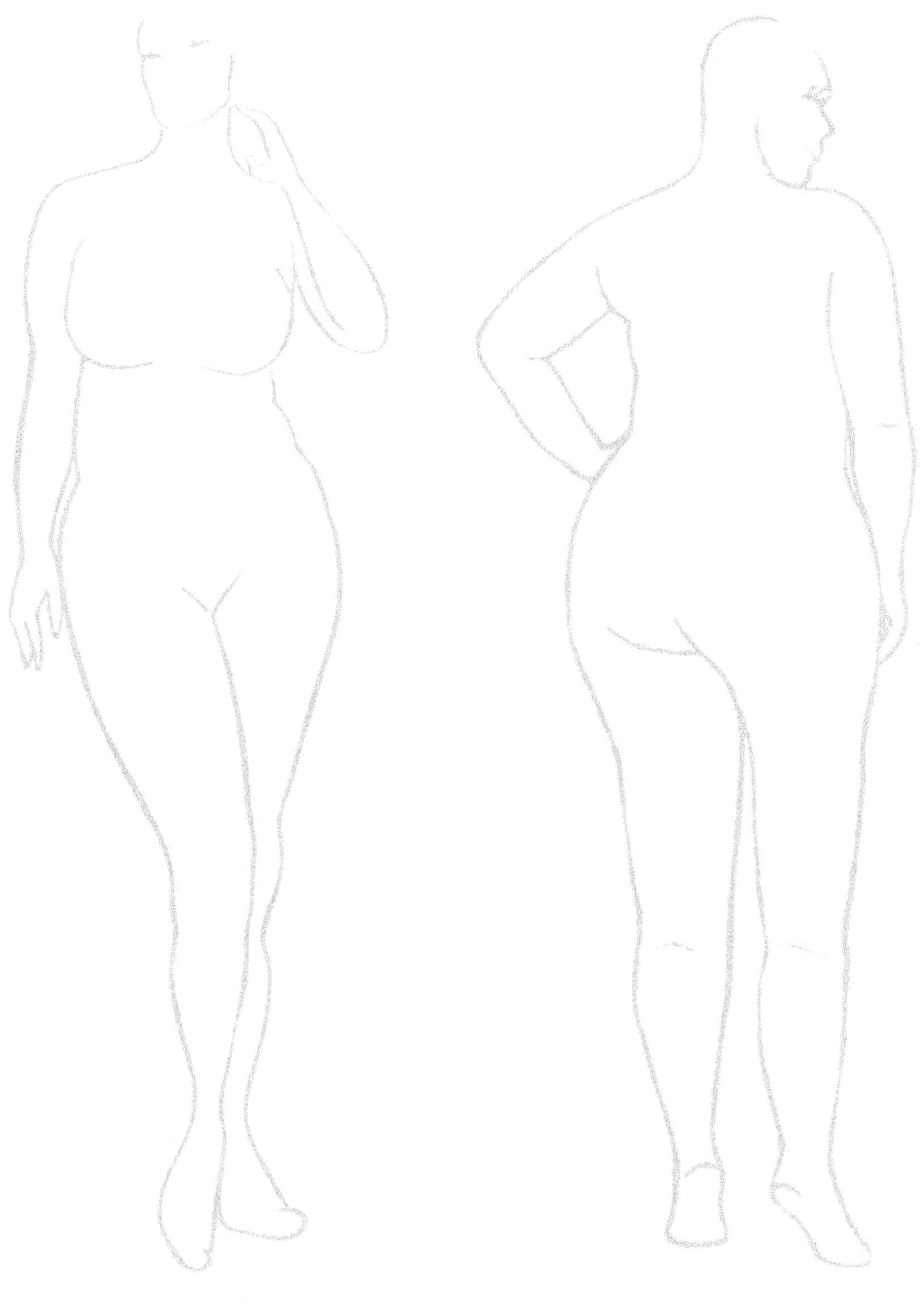

NOTES

NOTES

NOTES

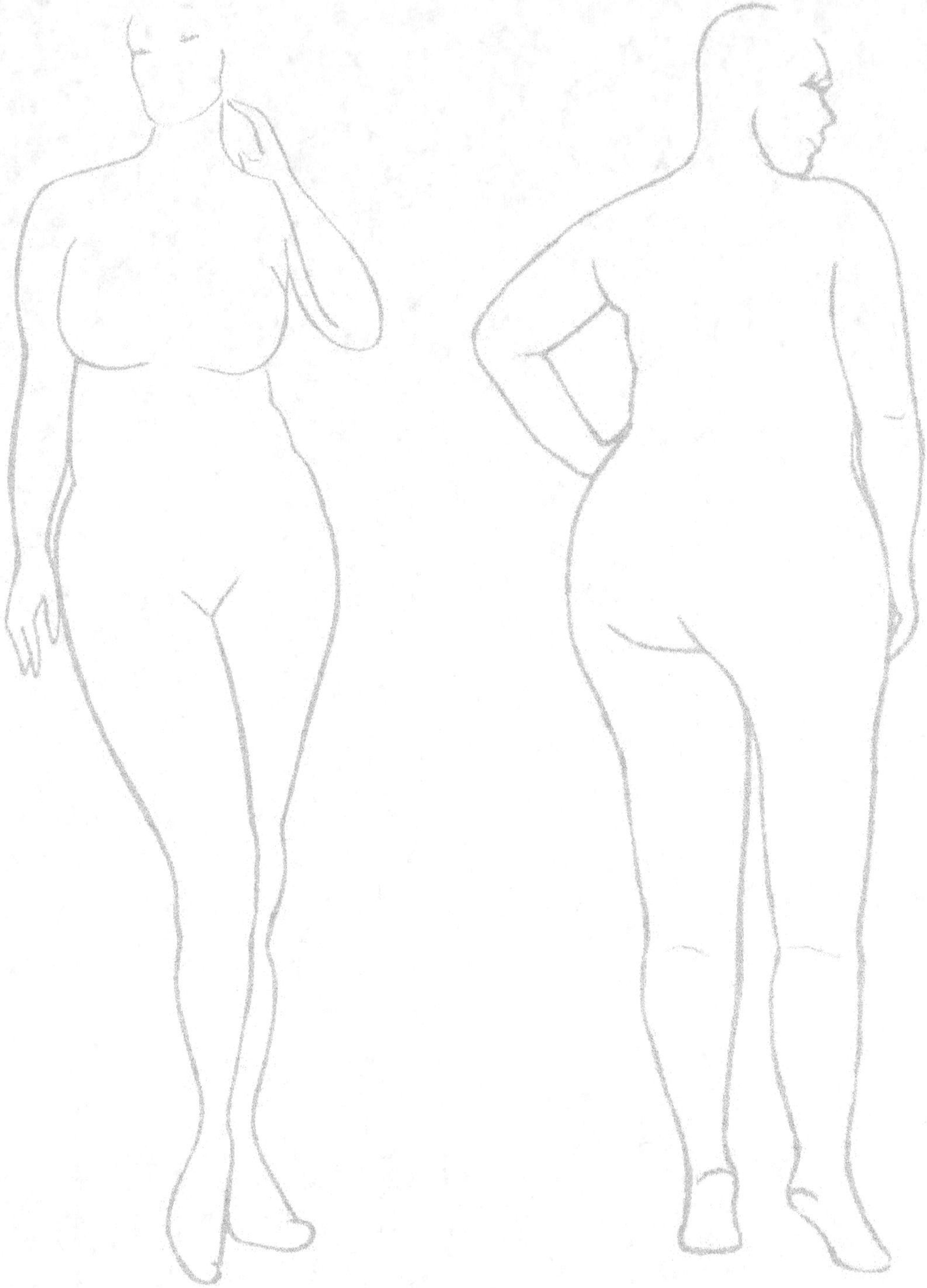

NOTES

NOTES

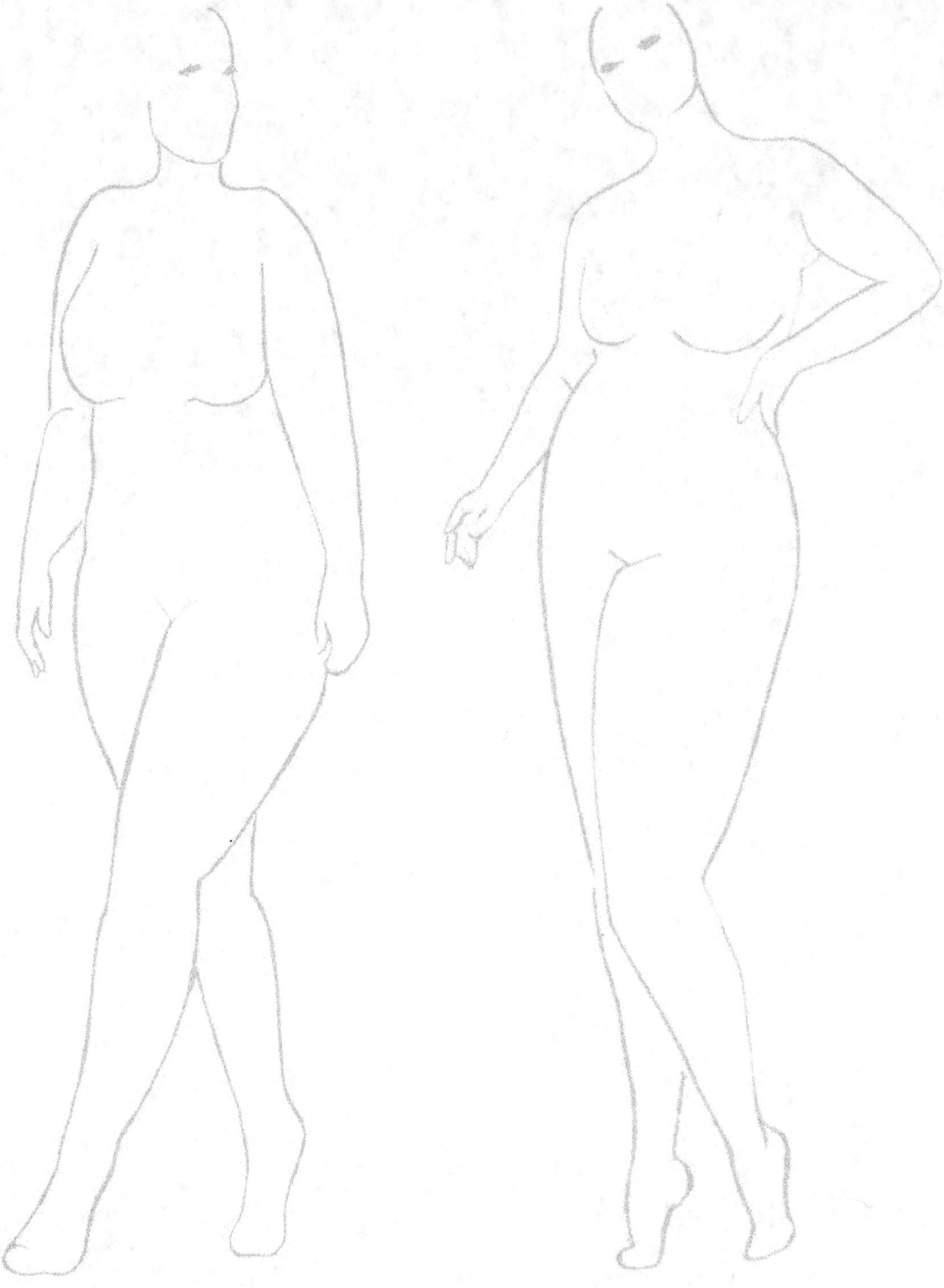

NOTES

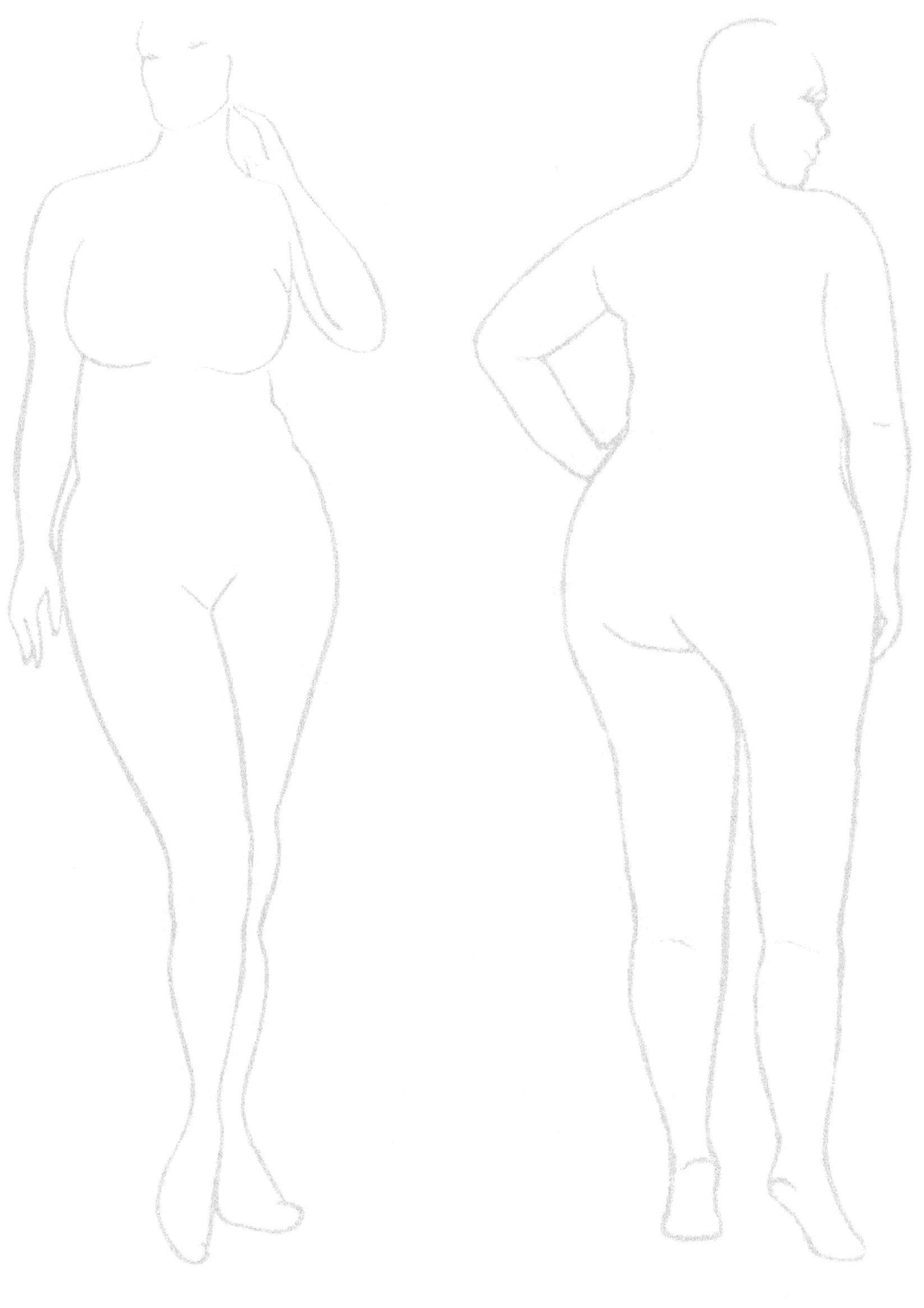

NOTES

NOTES

NOTES

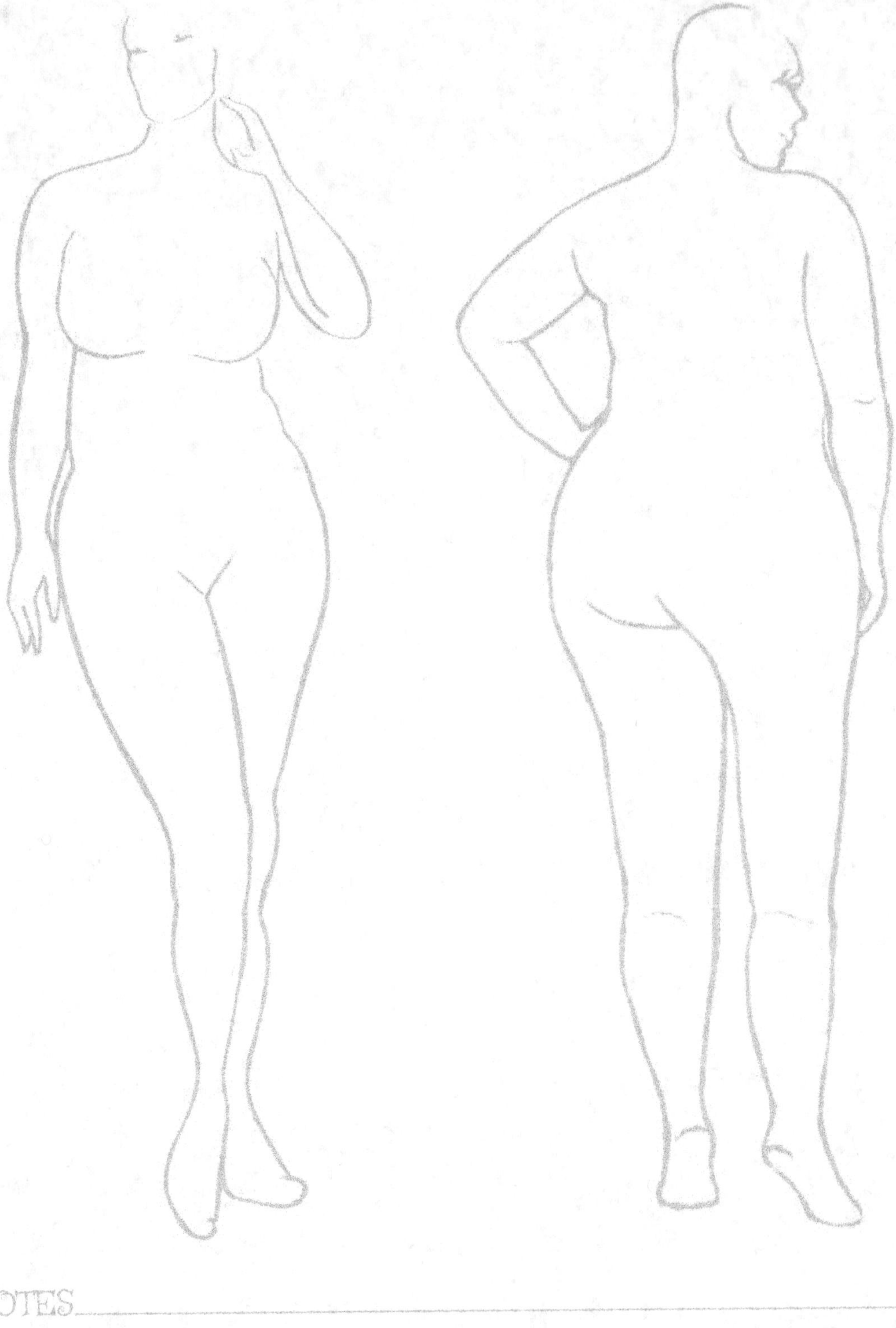

NOTES

NOTES

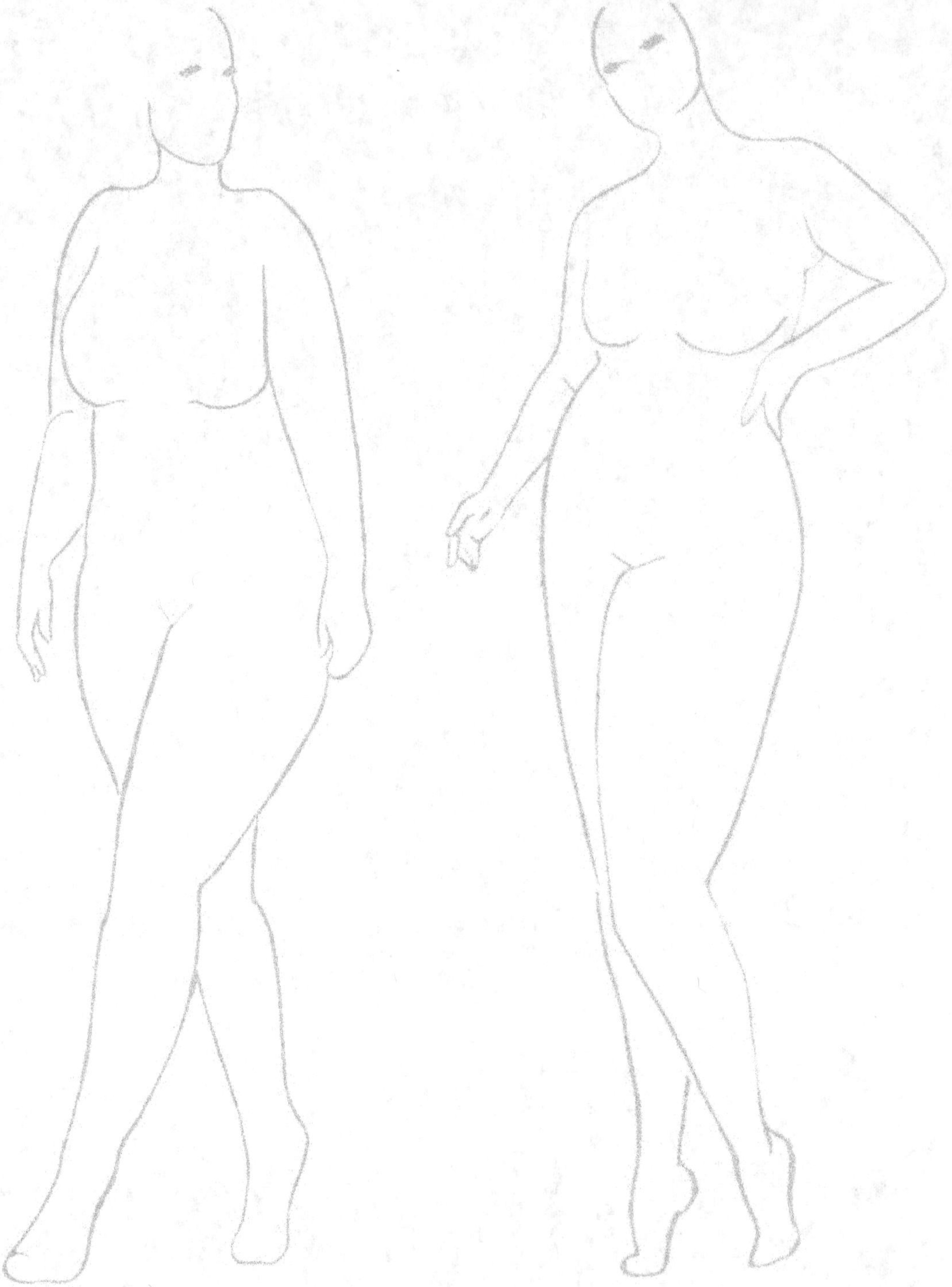

NOTES

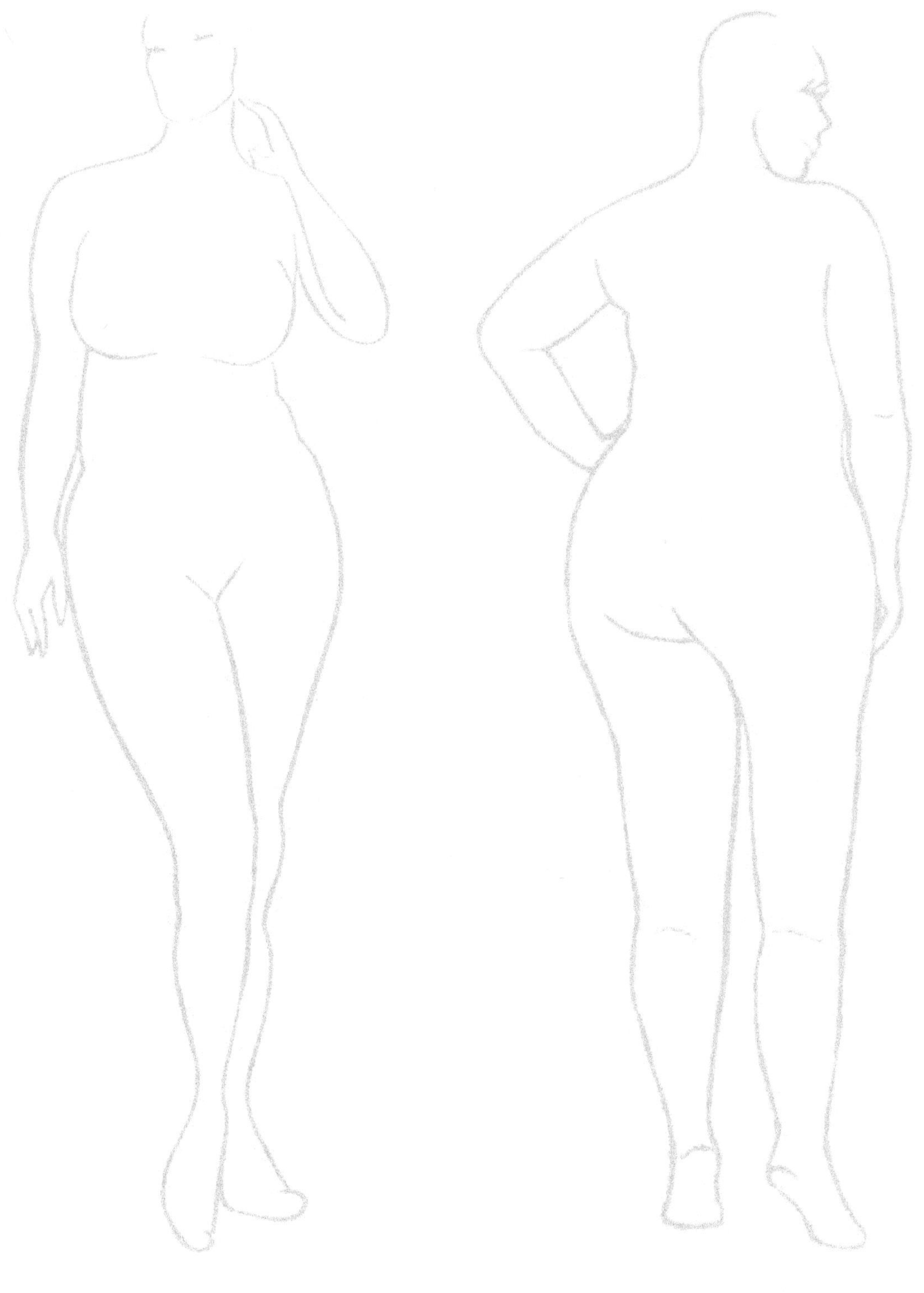

NOTES

NOTES

NOTES

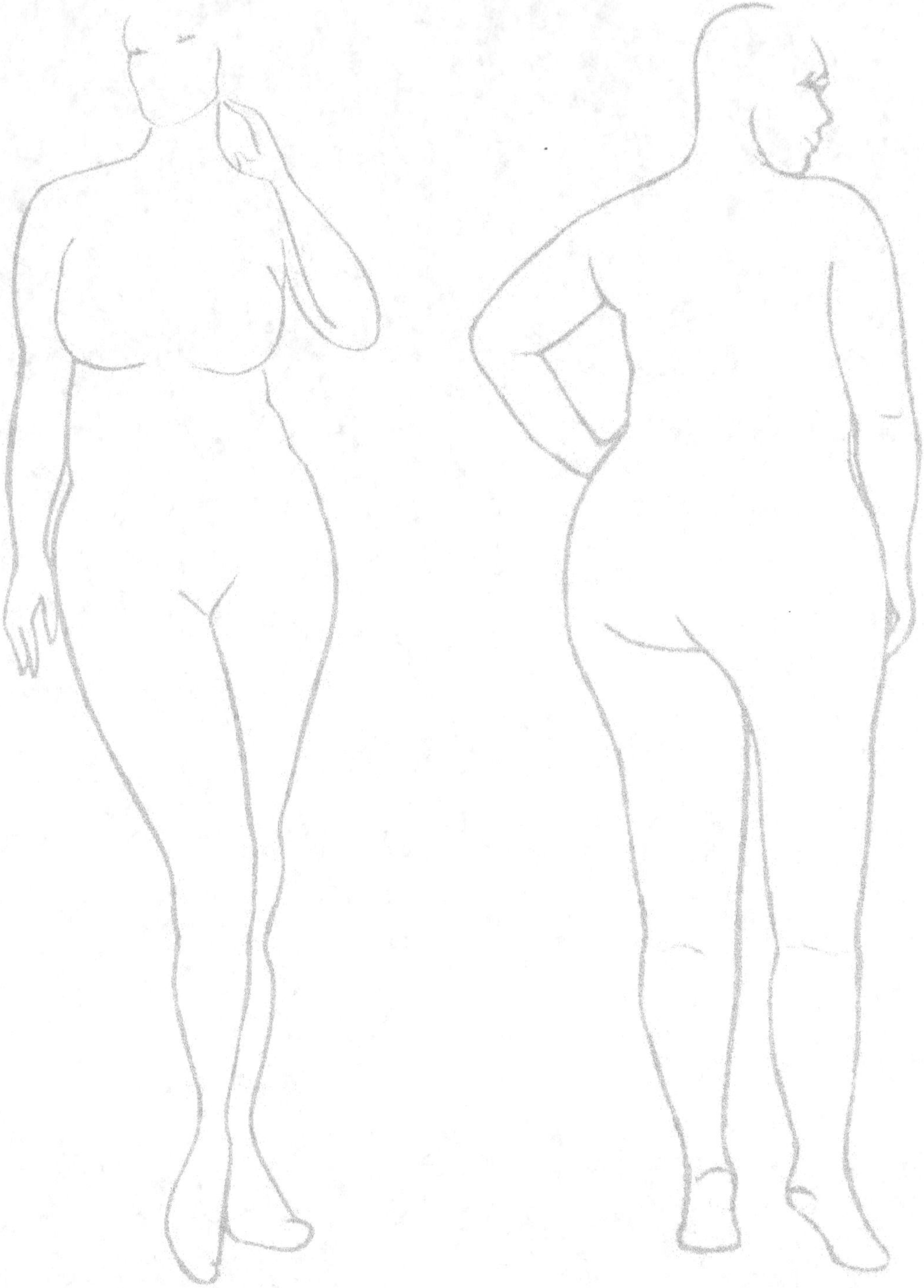

NOTES____

____

____

____

____

____

NOTES

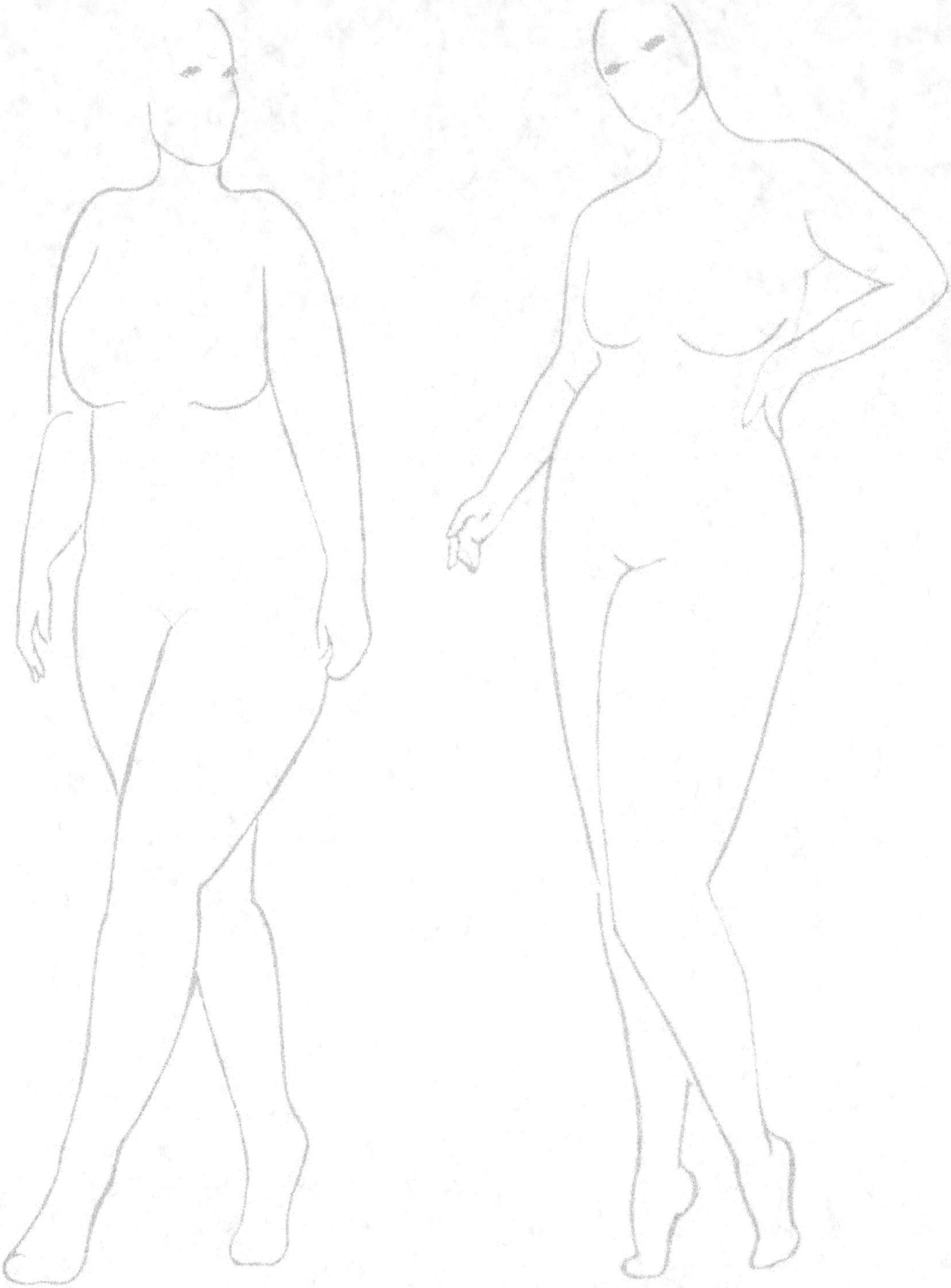

NOTES

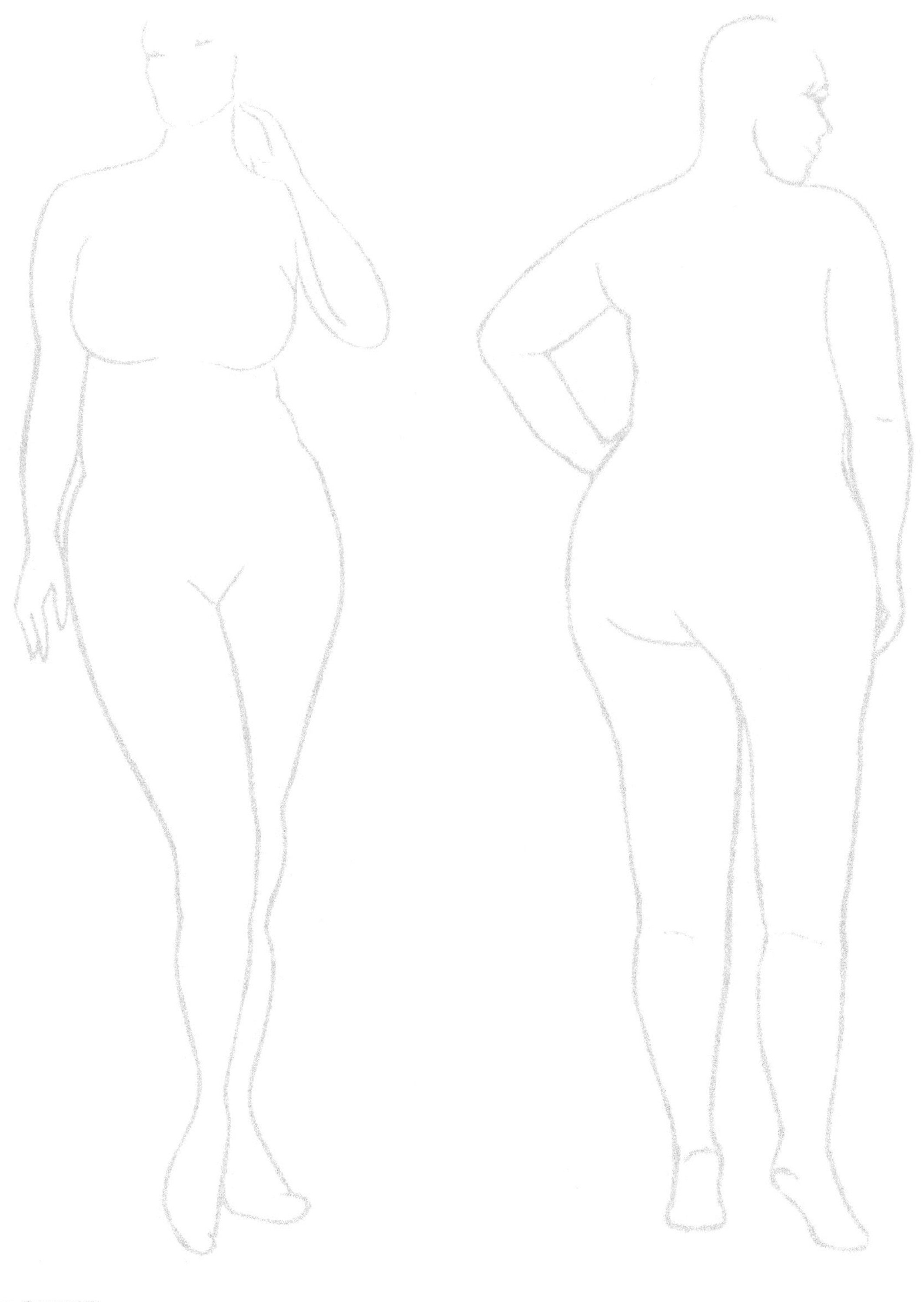

NOTES

NOTES

NOTES

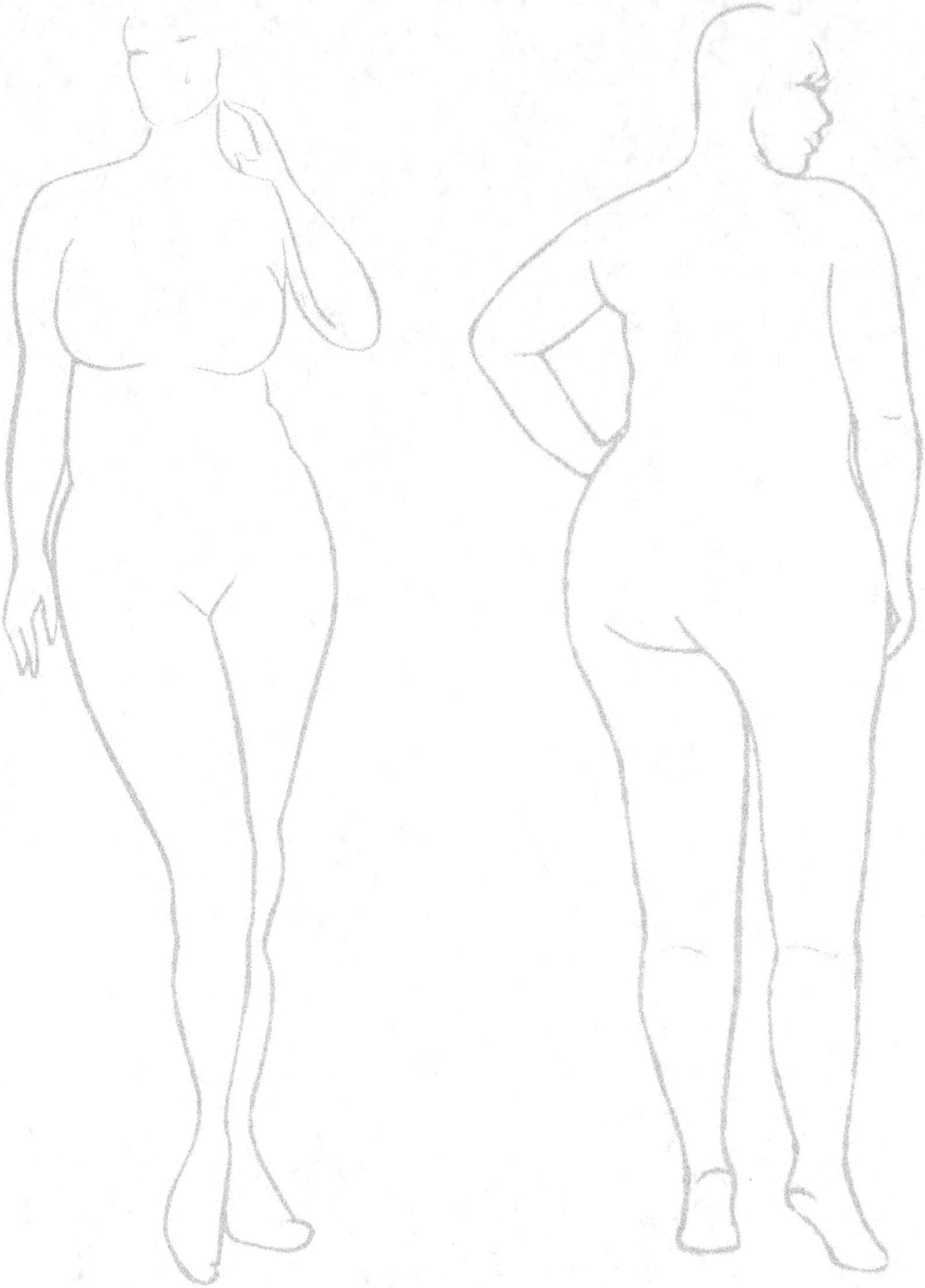

NOTES

NOTES

NOTES____

____

____

____

____

____

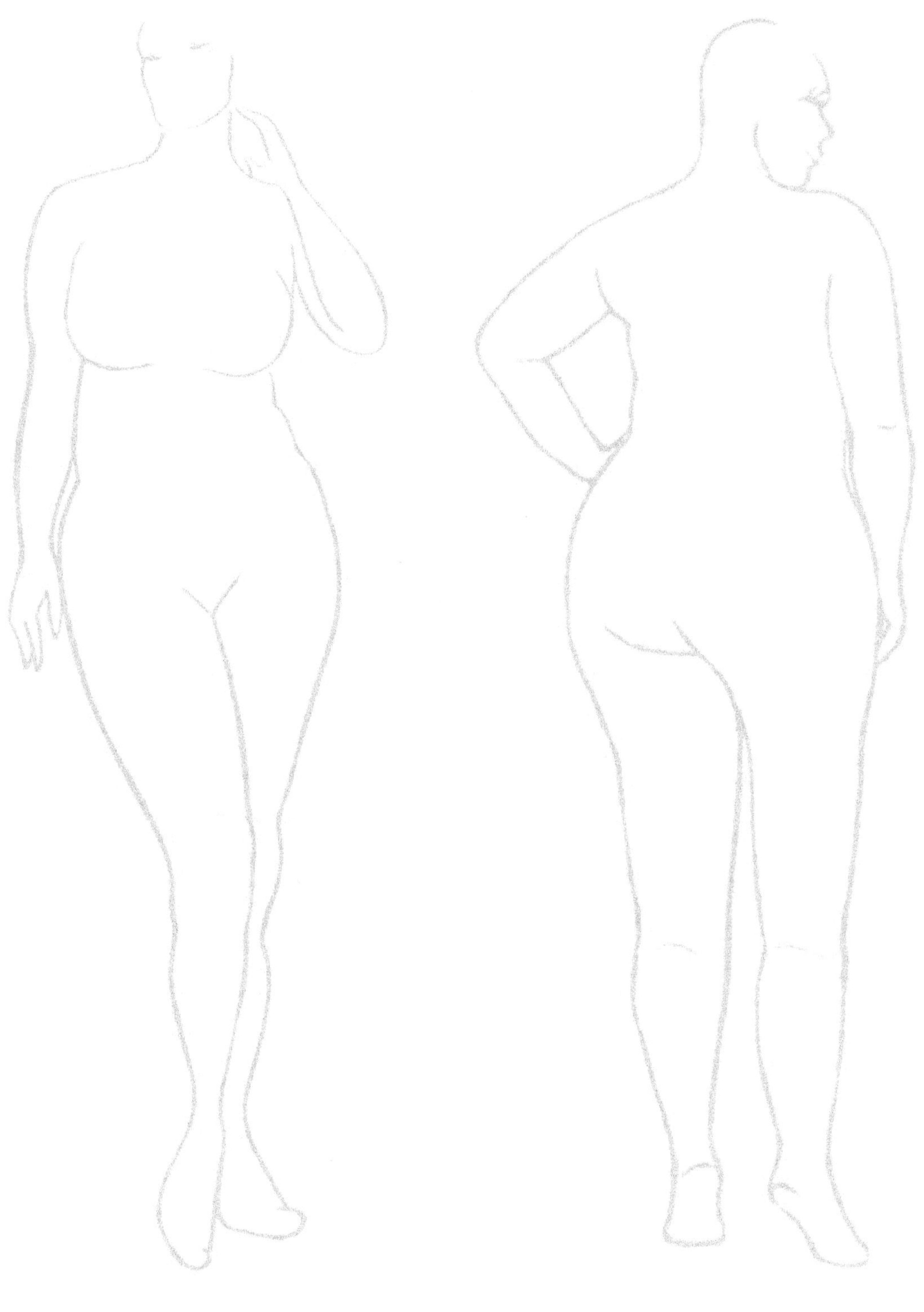

NOTES

NOTES

NOTES

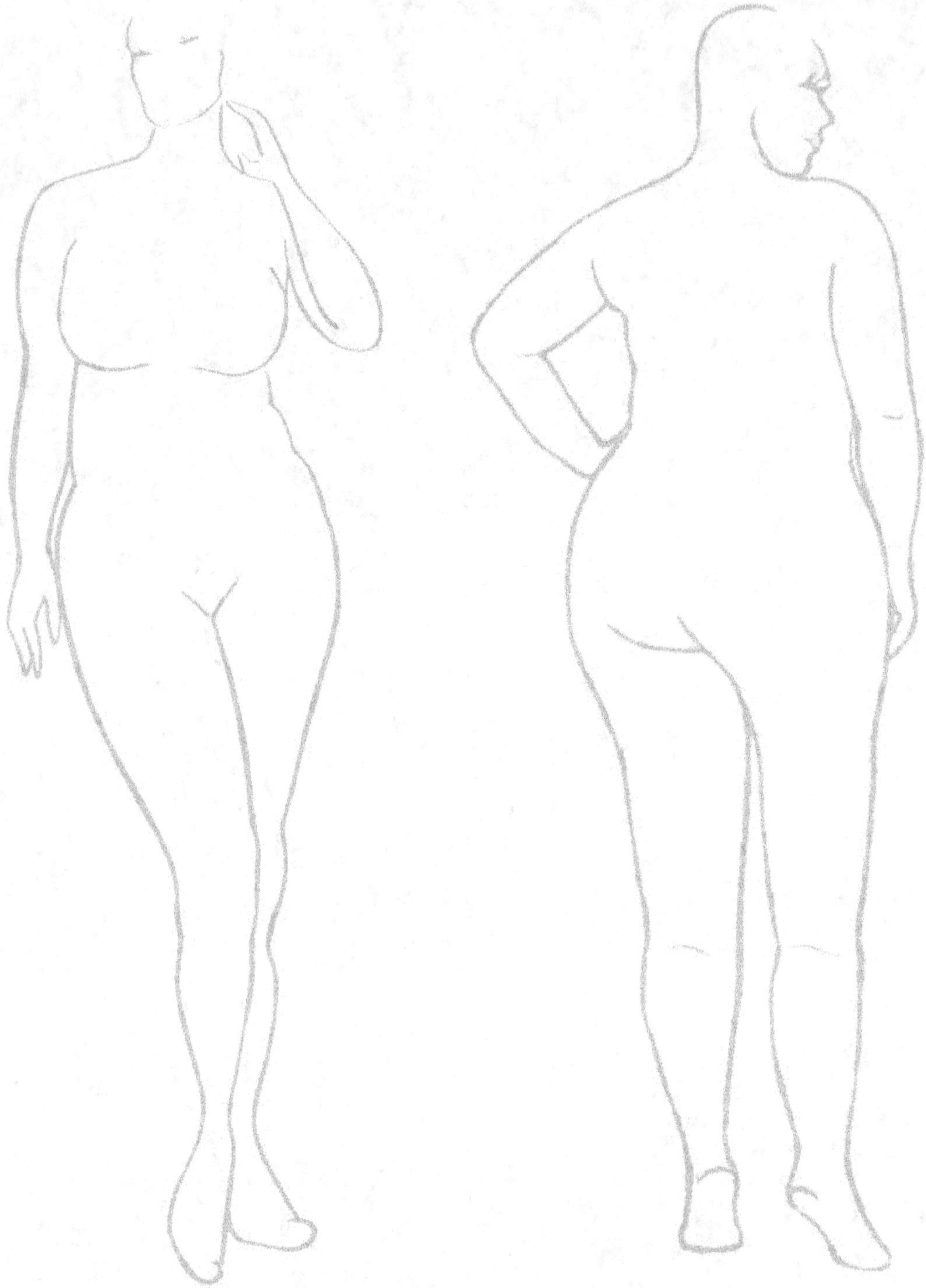

NOTES______________________________________

____

____

____

____

____

NOTES

NOTES_______________________________________

____

____

____

____

____

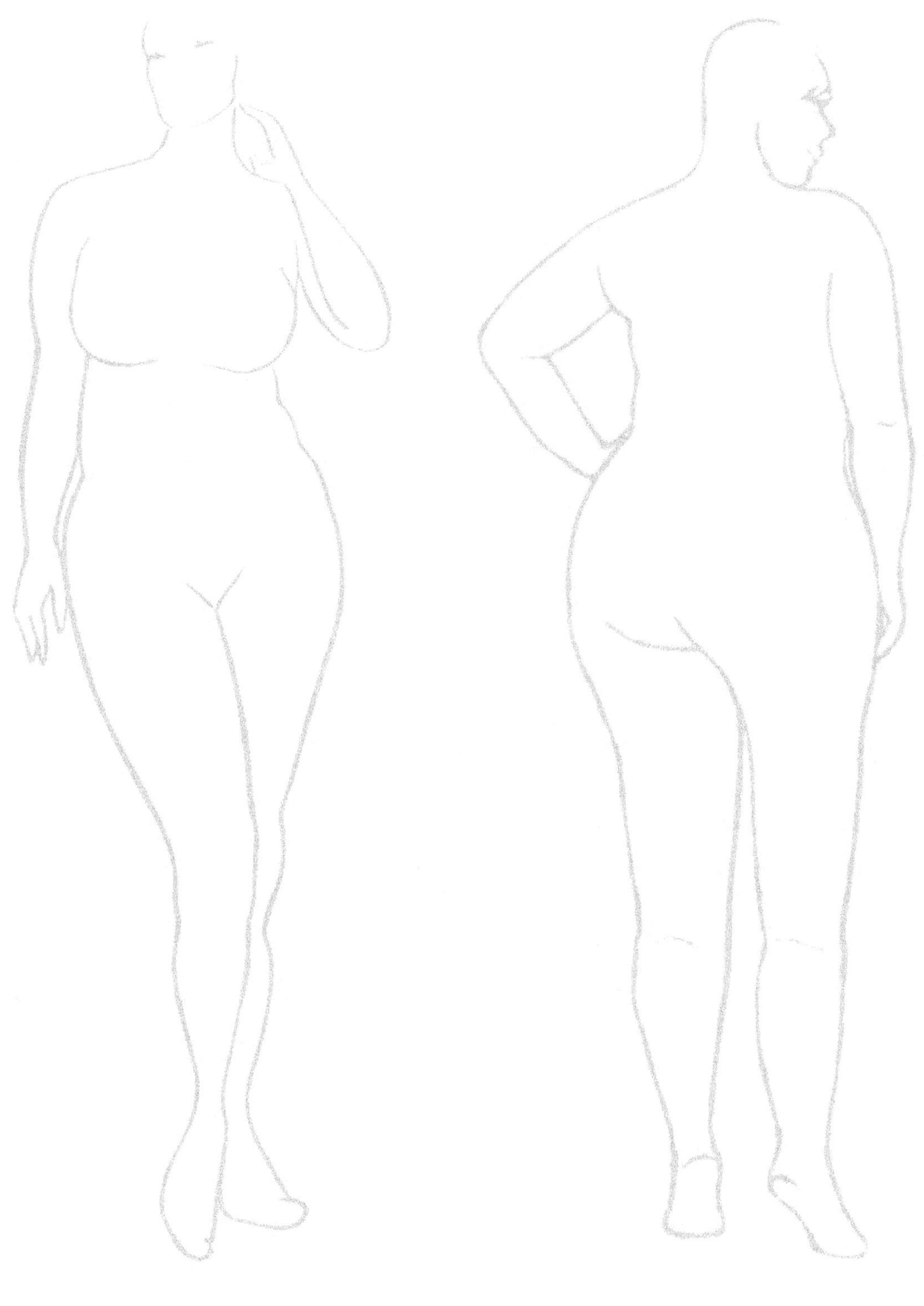

NOTES

NOTES

NOTES

NOTES

NOTES

www.ingramcontent.com/pod-product-compliance
Lightning Source LLC
Chambersburg PA
CBHW080836160726
47999CB00009B/2914